The Age
of Feudalism

The Age of Feudalism

John Davenport

LUCENT BOOKS

An imprint of Thomson Gale, a part of The Thomson Corporation

Detroit • New York • San Francisco • New Haven, Conn. • Waterville, Maine • London

LIBRARY OF CONGRESS CATALOGING-IN-PUBLICATION DATA

Davenport, John, 1960–
The age of feudalism / By John Davenport.
    p. cm. — (World history series)
Includes bibliographical references and index.
ISBN-13: 978-1-59018-649-7 (hardcover)
1. Feudalism—Europe—History—Juvenile literature. 2. Feudalism—History—Juvenile literature. 3. Middle Ages—Juvenile literature. 4. State, The—Juvenile literature. I. Title.

D131.D38 2007
940.1—dc22

2007015981

ISBN-10: 1-59018-649-4

Printed in the United States of America

Contents

Foreword

Each year, on the first day of school, nearly every history teacher faces the task of explaining why his or her students should study history. Many reasons have been given. One is that lessons exist in the past from which contemporary society can benefit and learn. Another is that exploration of the past allows us to see the origins of our customs, ideas, and institutions. Concepts such as democracy, ethnic conflict, or even things as trivial as fashion or mores, have historical roots.

Reasons such as these impress few students, however. If anything, these explanations seem remote and dull to young minds. Yet history is anything but dull. And therein lies what is perhaps the most compelling reason for studying history: History is filled with great stories. The classic themes of literature and drama—love and sacrifice, hatred and revenge, injustice and betrayal, adversity and overcoming adversity—fill the pages of history books, feeding the imagination as well as any of the great works of fiction do.

The story of the Children's Crusade, for example, is one of the most tragic in history. In 1212 Crusader fever hit Europe. A call went out from the pope that all good Christians should journey to Jerusalem to drive out the hated Muslims and return the city to Christian con-trol. Heeding the call, thousands of children made the journey. Parents bravely allowed many children to go, and entire communities were inspired by the faith of these small Crusaders. Unfortunately, many boarded ships captained by slave traders, who enthusiastically sold the children into slavery as soon as they arrived at their destination. Thousands died from disease, exposure, and starvation on the long march across Europe to the Mediterranean Sea. Others perished at sea.

Another story, from a modern and more familiar place, offers a soul-wrenching view of personal humiliation but also the ability to rise above it. Hatsuye Egami was one of 110,000 Japanese Americans sent to internment camps during World War II. "Since yesterday we Japanese have ceased to be human beings," he wrote in his diary. "We are numbers. We are no longer Egamis, but the number 23324. A tag with that number is on every trunk, suitcase and bag. Tags, also, on our breasts." Despite such dehumanizing treatment, most internees worked hard to control their bitterness. They created workable communities inside the camps and demonstrated again and again their loyalty as Americans.

These are but two of the many stories from history that can be found in the pages of the Lucent Books World History series. All World History titles rely on sound research and verifiable evidence, and all give students a clear sense of time, place, and chronology through maps and timelines as well as text.

All titles include a wide range of authoritative perspectives that demonstrate the complexity of historical interpretation and sharpen the reader's critical thinking skills. Formally documented quotations and annotated bibliographies enable students to locate and evaluate sources, often instantaneously via the Internet, and serve as valuable tools for further research and debate.

Finally, Lucent's World History titles present rousing good stories, featuring vivid primary source quotations drawn from unique, sometimes obscure sources such as diaries, public records, and contemporary chronicles. In this way, the voices of participants and witnesses as well as important biographers and historians bring the study of history to life. As we are caught up in the lives of others, we are reminded that we too are characters in the ongoing human saga, and we are better prepared for our own roles.

432
St. Patrick goes to Ireland to convert its people to Christianity.

814
Using an Indian system, Muslims begin using zero in equations.

1000
The Chinese perfect the recipe for gunpowder. Leif Eriksson discovers America.

850
Jews in Germany invent the Yiddish language.

570
The prophet Muhammad, the founder of Islam, is born.

300	400	500	600	700	800	900	1000

600
The first books are printed in China using a block-printing method.

810
A Muslim Iranian scientist invents algebra.

900
The first true castles appear in Europe.

978
Encyclopedias appear in China.

1364
The Aztecs found their capital city of Tenochtitlán, on the site that is today occupied by the capital of Mexico, Mexico City.

1453
Johannes Gutenberg uses a printing press for the first time in Europe. The book he produces becomes the world's all-time best seller, the Bible.

1100   1200   1300   1400   1500   1600

1155
The Mongol leader Genghis Khan is born.

1441
The Portuguese begin the global slave trade by kidnapping and selling a group of West Africans.

1451
The explorers Christopher Columbus and Amerigo Vespucci are born. The New World will be introduced to Europe as "America," Vespucci's given name in its feminine form.

1492
Columbus makes landfall in the New World on the first of four voyages across the Atlantic.

1500
Traditional date of the beginning of the European High Renaissance.

Rome, A.D. 410

Most people in Rome knew it was coming. They had followed the news of the invaders' advance for months. Each day brought fresh tales of defeat, slaughter, and ruin. Throughout the city, Romans whispered to one another that "they" would soon arrive at the gates. Any day now, Rome would suffer the fate that had befallen so many other imperial cities. The barbarians were on the move. Visigoths were marching down the Italian peninsula, sweeping aside all before them. No one was safe; no city or town was secure. The empire had given way. To the Romans it seemed like the entire world was coming to an end.

The term "barbarians" refers to groups of people that are considered inferior by others. The Visigoths were one of these groups considered to be barbarians. Led by their great warrior-king, Alaric, the Visigoths had stormed into the Roman Empire and fought their way toward the majestic city of Rome. A vast barbarian army was heading toward the capital of the Western world in the year 410. Alaric's men cut a fearful swath of death and destruction as they marched along. According to one Roman writer, "[the Visigoths] destroyed all the cities they captured . . . they killed all the people, as many as came their way, both old and young alike, sparing neither women nor children."[1] Terrible as it was, this was only a preview of what awaited Rome.

Within the city itself, panic grew. The Roman senate, quaking in fear, tried to pay the barbarians to stay away; the senators offered their adversaries gold and jewels if they left Rome in peace. The barbarians refused. Alaric came, determined to enter the imperial capital in triumph. When he and his soldiers finally arrived, the senate ordered the city gates shut against him. It did no good. Alaric's warriors laid siege to the city and broke through the gates on August 24. Enraged by Rome's attempt to stop him, Alaric turned his men loose on Rome's citizens. The Visigoths proceeded to ransack Rome in a six-day rampage of looting, pillaging, and murder. It was the first time in eight hundred years that an enemy had rampaged through the city's cobblestone streets. No one had done so since the Gauls, during their invasion of Italy way back in 390 B.C. when Rome was still in its infancy. Alaric's feat thus signaled the beginning of the end of the Roman Empire.

The Roman World

Politically, socially, culturally, and economically, Rome had served as the West's focal point for centuries. No one could remember a time when the empire had not dominated European life. Even when it came to religion, Rome stood at the center. Since the year 313, Christianity had been protected under Roman law; it became the sole legal religion eighty-two years later. Rome, then, functioned as the capital of two kingdoms, one of humans and one of God. Millions of people from the lowest reaches of the Danube River to the windswept hills of northern Britain built their lives around Roman power and authority. Suddenly, in 410, that power and authority could no longer be depended upon. Instability and confusion descended across the empire. Daily life became uncertain, and the future was darkened by instability.

Alaric, king of the Visigoths, invaded and raided Rome. This act signaled the beginning of the end of the Roman Empire.

Many of the empire's inhabitants thrown into turmoil lived in cities and towns. Urban life under the Romans had attracted people with its promise of safety and material comfort. Residents were drawn to urban centers by their prosperity and convenience. But now, with waves of invaders rolling in from the east, cities with their wealth, industry, and commerce became targets of often bloody barbarian raids. Attention, therefore, turned to the countryside. People began to depend upon the villages that were clustered along the fringes of the large rural estates maintained by the Roman elite. As the empire slowly disintegrated, these estates grew in importance. They gradually became hubs of social, economic, and political activity. The estates even offered some limited physical protection to the families that depended upon them. Rome might no longer be capable of guaranteeing order and security, people thought, but perhaps the local nobility could. Many of the functions of imperial officials, over time, were assumed by estate owners. Estate owners organized both the political and economic lives of the people. At the same time, the European economy shifted toward a concept of wealth based on land rather than money. Gold was just shiny metal, but land produced food. Grain supplies, among other food stocks, had been seriously diminished by the barbarian raids. Farm output had been reduced, and food shortages had become more common. Farm land, thus, took on a new prominence. The men who possessed it, and so could feed the people from it, took center stage in an emerging economic order based on the accumulation and protection of the soil itself.

The Great Estates

Access to land had always been an issue in Rome. Since the earliest days of its history, Rome's political leaders had tried to prevent the concentration of land in the hands of the elite. During the days of the old Roman republic (509 B.C.–27 B.C.), land ownership meant that a man had a real stake in the political health and prosperity of Rome. Land made a man into a taxpayer and thus a better kind of citizen than the landless worker. It made a man independent and allowed him to determine his own future without relying on anyone else. With his own land, a man had a ready source of food and property he could sell or rent out, if times got hard. The image of the hardy, self-sufficient Roman farmer working his patch of land was cherished widely.

The ideal, however, was often quite different from the reality. In practice, no amount of republican fantasizing could prevent the accumulation of land by the elite and the appearance of huge rural estates belonging to a noble minority. Vast estates sprang up throughout the Roman world, producing everything from grain to grapes. These estates were worked by armies of slaves. Over time, more land was owned by fewer people, inflating the importance of the country estates in the scheme of daily life. The estate owners, always prominent figures in Roman society and politics, took on new responsibilities. Eventually, they became something like mini-governors of the areas surrounding their holdings. As the Roman system, at all levels, dissolved in the fourth and fifth centuries, this process accelerated. Estate owners were transformed into providers, protectors, and administrators. The nobility came to exercise new powers over a new class of dependents. Land, wealth, dominance, and submission—the core of the arrangement that would become known as feudalism—began to take shape.

Just in Time

The system of relations that began to form around the estates appeared just in time. Year by year, mile by mile, the Roman Empire retreated in the face of relentless barbarian advances. The immigrants, or invaders, depending upon the manner in which they crossed the imperial borders, hailed from the East. Usually traversing either the Rhine or Danube frontiers, they pressed in from every direction. Attempting to cope with the newcomers, Rome split itself in two in the late fourth century. The Roman leadership felt that it would be easier to defend two smaller empires than a single large one. The East-West division did nothing to stem the tide of change. By the year 476 the borders were breaking up. Roman governors and provincial officers fled toward the imperial center. Large portions of Europe were left to fend for themselves. The Roman army, once invincible, lost major and minor battles alike. In many instances the imperial legions that remained

A map of western Europe, circa A.D. 500, shows the movements of various barbarian tribes.

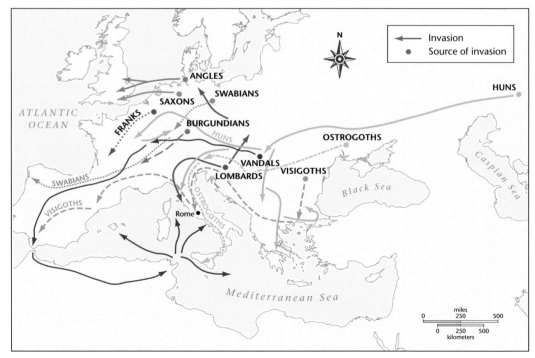

in the field were filled with barbarian recruits and foreign mercenaries (soldiers for hire). On the rare occasion of a "Roman" victory, the soldiers who did the fighting were often barbarians recruited by Rome.

Denied the organization of Rome, public services in most areas simply disappeared. Roads went without maintenance; water supplies dwindled where they were not already contaminated. Public buildings and marketplaces fell into disrepair. Threatened by barbarian raiders, cities lost inhabitants rapidly. Those people who sought refuge in the country were confronted by a bewildering array of immigrant groups that seemed to be swarming over the land. Visigoths, Ostrogoths, Vandals, Huns, Angles, Saxons, Avars, Alans, and dozens of other tribal peoples arrived yearly in ever-greater numbers. Sometimes they blended into the existing Roman society; other times, the barbarians resorted to violence to establish themselves in their new homes. Regardless of how it was happening, the old order was dying.

Understanding the necessity, the estate owners seized the opportunity. They threw out the traditional model of social and political relations that relied on a strong imperial government in Rome and replaced it with a feudal one that put them in charge. As one historian has explained, the newly empowered nobles "fortified their mansions and kept private armies."[2] They negotiated with local communities, trading protection for the labor of the town's citizens. The nobility gathered up as much land as it could, taking over small farms whose owners, soon to be called serfs, "lost their freedom, [but] gained security, a fair bargain in a tottering world."[3]

The final blow to the Roman world came in 476. That year, the last Roman emperor stepped down and was replaced by a barbarian tribal chieftain who made himself king of Italy. The Western Roman Empire soon crumbled into a dizzying and ever-shifting patchwork of barbarian kingdoms. The ancient forms of organization faded and were replaced by a new system based on the relationship between people of various classes and the land itself. The great landholders of the post-Roman world would owe their loyalty and service to kings, just as people below the estate owners would owe theirs to those above them. The age of feudalism had dawned.

Chapter One

Barbarian Kingdoms

As the sixth century opened, the Eastern Roman Empire was intact, but its western counterpart had been shattered. Rome no longer dominated Europe; the city was now just another city. Italy, once the domain of the Caesars, became home to Ostrogoths and Huns. Soon the Lombards would be its masters. Roman Gaul had been taken over by the Franks, a tribal group that came to call their new land France. Far to the north, Angles, Saxons, and Jutes occupied Roman Britain, bringing with them Germanic customs and the language that would someday become English. Spain, by the year 500, belonged to the Visigoths; the Vandals claimed North Africa. Alans, Avars, and Slavs filtered into central Europe and made it theirs.

No matter where one looked, the new order of things was managed by barbarian rulers, chieftains, and kings who picked up where the Romans left off. The eastern emperor tried to keep some remnants of Roman society alive, but his power stopped at the old border with the West. Even inside the Eastern Empire, Roman ways were disappearing. Greek influences had always competed with Latin ones in the East; with the fall of Rome, the former were winning out. The imperial capital, Constantinople, had once been the Greek city of Byzantium. It now began to revert to its original Greek form. Thus, the eastern Romans were rarely called Romans. Instead, most people simply referred to them as Greeks or, more formally, Byzantines. The eastern Roman territorial possessions were called the Byzantine Empire. West and East, the word "Roman" and all it stood for became an antique term, less a symbol of power than a synonym for collapse.

The Barbarian Way
Everywhere, except for the Byzantine East, barbarians were in command. Yet there

was no single way to be barbarian. The Roman Empire had been diverse, but barbarian Europe was much more so. Each of the tribal groups that replaced the Romans was vastly different from its neighbors. Germans were not Goths. Lombards had nothing in common with Franks. Anglo-Saxons were completely different from Vandals. The barbarian label, in fact, masked a wide range of political and social differences and many ways of life. As the historian Antonio Santosuosso has put it, the "idea that all barbarians shared a common cultural, physical, political, and linguistic origin"[4] was a creation of writers who lived centuries after the fact.

Still, there were some qualities that linked the tribes together, no matter if they came from Germany, Scandinavia, or central Asia. To begin with, the political structures they used to govern themselves were adaptable. Kings and chieftains, who had to fight for their positions, struggled for power with the warrior elite who served them. Authority, therefore, was highly decentralized, and the extent of any single king's influence was limited. Barbarian leaders, in other words, never exercised total or uncontested control over their people. This meant that the village or farm community served as the focal point of daily affairs, political and otherwise. This was because tribal leaders, other than the local ones who took ownership of the old Roman estates, were located so far from the individual communities or villages. There was little contact between these tribal leaders and the citizens.

Without strong monarchies, capital cities occupied

The barbarians focused most of their economic attention on food production. The cultivation of staple crops, namely wheat, was the primary occupation of the vast majority of Europeans.

The first barbarian king of Italy, Odoacer, faces his troops.

a small place in the barbarian scheme of things. Indeed, cities as a whole were far less important than they had been in the empire. Politically unimportant, urban centers became economically useless as trade slowed after 500. Large-scale manufacturing ground to a halt, and daily transactions for essential goods were completed on a barter basis. If someone needed a cow, say, he might trade for it using something he had, such as a few chickens. Luxury items were limited to occasional pieces of jewelry and clothing for the elite. The barbarians, in fact, concentrated most of their economic attention on food production. The cultivation of staple crops, namely wheat, was the primary occupation of the vast majority of Europeans. Bread was literally life. Barbarian society, therefore, was not only local but agrarian as well. Thus the farm became more important than the city.

Rural, agrarian, local, and decentralized, the barbarian way in general produced institutions that were perfectly suited to a fragmented post-Roman Europe. Because control was concentrated in local communities, decisions could be made quickly and more efficiently; people could be protected and fed better. Of course, there were many variations on this theme and quite a few unique patterns appeared across the continent. Yet, overall, the barbarian system could be summed up as one in which competing centers of power organized the lives of de-urbanized people living in villages clustered around rural estates. The local elite supervised and defended the peasantry, or common people, while the peasants grew food for the elite and themselves. Europe's new masters much more boldly drew feudalism's outlines, which had been sketched lightly during Roman times.

Clovis and the Franks

The barbarian chieftains who oversaw this new economy and social order were a tough lot. They had to be if they hoped to build kingdoms on political foundations weakened by the presence of a quarreling, jealous warrior elite. Among the toughest was Clovis I of the Franks. Known to his own people as Chlodwig (which means "noble warrior"), Clovis was described by an early Christian bishop as *"magnus et pugnator egregius,"*[5] a great and magnificent fighter.

Born from a long line of Frankish leaders, Clovis rose to power through warfare. When he became chieftain of the Franks in 482, Clovis was only fifteen years old. To prove himself to his followers, Clovis launched a series of successful attacks against other barbarian tribes. He further improved his standing in 496 when he converted to Christianity. The church, as the last tie to the Roman Empire and Europe's only religious institution, exerted a good deal of influence in social and political affairs. By tying himself to it, Clovis put God and the legacy of the old empire on his side. The church, for its part, did not object to having a fierce warrior as its defender.

Clovis's marriage to a Christian princess cemented the bond between the Frankish

chief and the church. Bolstered by religion, Clovis initiated armed campaigns against the Burgundians and Germans. Both groups were Arians, Christians who did not accept that Christ was the son of God. This made them enemies of the

Clovis I was only fifteen years old when he became chieftain of the Franks and proved himself by launching a series of attacks against other barbarian tribes.

church in Rome. Clovis, in defeating these tribes, helped the church extend its reach deep into northern Europe. He was rewarded with huge land grants that might have been stitched together into a true kingdom if Clovis had not died suddenly in 511. His sons divided their father's territory, and their sons did likewise. Instead of one France, there were now many, each one its own little world.

This suited the Franks, though, and they devised a system to organize the lands Clovis gave to them. Clovis had never been a king, in the modern sense of the word, nor were the men who came after him. Rather than monarchs, Frankish leaders in the barbarian period were more like firsts among noble equals. The elite respected and usually obeyed them, but the kings' prerogatives were sharply limited. Frankish kings, in practice, handed over most functions of government to the upper nobility, which passed responsibility farther down to their counterparts in the lesser nobility. At the end of the line were the local landowners who served as civil officials responsible for administration and military affairs. Everyone in the chain received service from below and accepted responsibility from above. Although not yet fully formed, the Frankish system was well on its way to becoming truly feudal in terms of obligation and duty.

The Ostrogoths and Lombards in Italy

While the Franks were busy organizing their leadership, forging links with the church, and crafting a feudal social order, the barbarians who had taken control of Italy were under assault. The Ostrogoths and a small population of Huns were on the defensive against a Byzantine emperor determined to retake Rome and revive the old united empire. Emperor Justinian I longed to rule an area that spanned Europe and the Middle East. According to one modern scholar, Justinian believed the city of Rome would be an indispensable part of it. Justinian planned a campaign against the barbarians in Italy because a "Roman Empire that did not include Rome was an absurdity; an Ostrogothic and Arian Kingdom that did, an abomination."[6]

Rome could not be left in the hands of barbarians, Justinian argued. For this reason, he sent two of his best generals, Belisarius and Narses, to Italy in 534 to get it back. Waging a ferocious campaign against the Ostrogoths and Huns, Belisarius and Narses systematically cleared them out of Italy, the ancient imperial heartland. But the war took a frightful toll. The Italian peninsula was devastated by the Byzantine invasion. Cities, or what was left of them, were in ruins; many large towns had been nearly destroyed. Where urban populations remained, a new menace appeared. Disease and famine swept up and down the length of Italy, striking particularly hard at Rome. By the mid-sixth century, the population of Rome had significantly decreased because of deaths due to disease and malnutrition. Of the 1 million residents who once lived in the city, scarcely fifty thousand remained.

The Benedictines

The first effort by the church to assume at least a portion of the responsibilities and power of the old Roman Empire was made in 529 by a clergyman named Benedict of Nursia. In that year he founded the monastery at Monte Cassino and with it the church's most enduring expression of its new social role. During the imperial period the church had relied on the Roman government to ensure its integration into everyday life. Without Rome, the church needed some vehicle to transport it across Europe and give it a place in local communities. Benedict's monasteries did that exceedingly well. While the Benedictines were not an official monastic order as such, they were bound together by adherence to the "Rule of Benedict," a strict code of behavior that regulated every aspect of a monk's existence. The rule gave instructions for religious conduct and also commanded that monasteries be self-sufficient and integrate themselves completely into the local society and economy. Benedictines assimilated themselves so thoroughly into Europe's far-flung agricultural settlements that people saw the monasteries as village fixtures. Other orders followed the Benedictine lead and built their monasteries so as to bring the church teachings and authority directly to the common folk.

Saint Benedict blesses Saint Marcus. The "Rule of Benedict" was a strict code of behavior that regulated every aspect of a monk's existence.

The Byzantines, unable to reconstruct what they had shattered, gave up power to the church. The bishop of Rome, known later as the pope, helped the Italian people in the wake of war. Revered as the agent of God on earth, the church quickly became a source of comfort, reassurance, and order. Its authority grew and moved outward from Rome. Monasteries sprang up throughout Italy, modeled on the great Benedictine monastery at Monte Cassino. Locally, the monasteries generated a sense that someone was in charge, in this case the pope through his representatives, the monks. They also transformed the church into a dominating political force. People seeking to rule Italy in the future would have to deal with the church either as an ally or a competitor. The Lombards were one of these peoples.

Originally from Germany, the Lombards conquered Italy in 568, filling a spot left vacant by both the Goths and the Byzantines. Although strong enough to accomplish this, the Lombards had neither the numbers nor the competence to rule effectively. They could seize but not hold on to power. The church recognized this and moved rapidly to exploit the Lombards' weaknesses. The pope made a great show of overlooking the fact that the Lombards were Arian Christians and offered, with seeming generosity, to exchange Italian estate titles for a division of local authority between Lombard nobles and church bishops. Pope Gregory the Great, for instance, used land titles to manipulate the Lombard aristocracy into giving him vast political privileges and setting aside valuable real estate for exclusive use by monasteries. The nobility and the clergy, therefore, blended at a very early date in Italy. Church and state mingled to a degree unseen in many other parts of feudal Europe to form a single elite sitting atop the Italian social ladder.

Visigoths and Vandals

During the course of the sixth century, the Lombards and Franks quickly adapted to the comforts and security of the emerging feudal order. The Visigoths and Vandals experienced a much more difficult transition from wandering tribes to settled peoples. Both groups had been among Rome's earliest barbarian enemies. The Visigoths, under a chieftain named Fritigern, first invaded Roman territory in the fourth century. It was a Visigothic army that annihilated a Roman force, killing an emperor in the process, at the battle of Adrianople in 378. Later, Alaric's Visigothic warriors stormed into Rome and sacked the city in 410.

The Vandals, whose native home was in northern Germany, migrated through what is today Russia before crossing the entire length of Europe on their way to Spain. Unfortunately for the Vandals, the Visigoths had already claimed Spain for themselves and were busily trying to organize a kingdom there. So the Vandals moved on, eventually crossing the Strait of Gibraltar to North Africa. The Vandal kingdom they subsequently established got off to a promising start. In 455 a Vandal fleet under the command of a chieftain named Gaiseric sailed for Rome. The

Vandals attack the city of Rome. Vandals experienced a difficult transition from wandering tribe to settled people.

fields and fought battles everywhere. The campaign also worsened the political and economic problems the Visigoths faced by bringing uncertainty to daily life. The Vandals fell on even harder times. Confronted by constant revolts by North African tribes and clans and torn by conflicts between their own leaders, the Vandals failed to move in any meaningful way toward basic stability, let alone any system as delicately balanced as feudalism. By the middle of the sixth century the Vandals were under direct Byzantine attack. They did not survive.

Vandals attacked the city and destroyed the vital port of Ostia. By 500 both the Vandals and the Visigoths seemed poised to mimic the successes of the Franks and Lombards.

The Visigoths fared better than the Vandals, but never achieved Frankish levels of order and organization. Forlorn attempts to revive the defunct Roman system of government led to economic and social stagnation. An invasion by Belisarius's Byzantine army in 554 disrupted daily life as armies trampled over farm

The English Kingdoms

The new arrangement, in which land equaled wealth and power and local nobles reigned supreme over a rural peasantry, failed to take root in North Africa, but it did so deeply and lastingly in England. Since the days of Julius Caesar, England had been a part of Rome. Over the centuries, Roman power expanded outward from the area surrounding the settlement of Londinium (London) all the way to the desolate moors near the border with Celtic Scotland. The Romans had taken great pride in bringing their traditions and customs to what they considered to be the edge of the world. The history of Roman Britain, however, ended abruptly in 442, when the last of the imperial legions was evacuated from the island. The Roman soldiers were almost immediately replaced by tribal warriors from Germany.

Angles, Saxons, Jutes, and Frisians began arriving in England around the middle of the fifth century, if not earlier. They brought with them a language and culture that overwhelmed those of the native Romano-Britons. Within a very short span of time the barbarian newcomers divided Britain into a collection of tiny interlocking kingdoms. Among the more stable and long lasting were Essex, Sussex, Wessex, Kent, Mercia, East Anglia, and Northumbia. Although linked by history, these kingdoms developed unique ways of life. Their general patterns of social and political evolution, however, were quite similar.

Kings and local nobles worked together to organize the legal and economic systems. Key here were notions about obligation and common defense that resembled closely those emerging on the European continent. In brief, peasants in Anglo-Saxon England owed service and loyalty to the nobility, who guided and protected their farm communities. Those lower in the hierarchy gave

The Origins of the Legend of King Arthur

The original population of the British Isles had been a diverse mix of Celtic groups. The Romans, often willfully ignorant of differences between the tribal peoples they fought and subdued, grouped them together haphazardly under the name Britons. They thus renamed the Celtic homeland Britannia and began an active program of Roman settlement and colonization. Celtic groups were expected either to accept the newcomers' presence or flee northward and westward into the wilds of Scotland and Wales. Those that chose to remain blended with their new Roman neighbors, creating a people known to history as the Romano-Britons. It was these Romano-Britons who met and at first resisted the Anglo-Saxon migrations of the fifth century. Out of the conflict between these two contestants for control of Britain arose the legend of King Arthur, the mythical king who defended his realm with the help of his trusty knights. Although the story has many variations and has been thoroughly revised via its numerous retellings over the centuries, the basic plotline has remained intact and reflects the confusion and fear that descended on Britain with the collapse of Roman rule.

Peasants gave their labor and produce to the nobility, who in turn guided and protected their farm communities.

Islam in Spain

Known at the time as Al-Andalus, Islamic Spain was unique in many ways. To begin with, although linked by religion to the rest of the Muslim world, Islamic Spain was quite different than other Muslim refuges. For example, its ruling dynasty, the Umayyads, no longer held power anywhere else in North Africa or the Middle East. Islamic Spain was also proudly multicultural. Its population, traditions, and customs reflected a blend of Arab, North African, and European influences. Drawing upon these, Spain became a center of art and knowledge. Libraries abounded; throughout Spain, scholars produced breakthrough research in science, mathematics, and medicine. Islamic men of learning also labored to translate the great books of ancient philosophy that had been almost forgotten by European descendents of the men who wrote them. Spain's architectural achievements such as the Alhambra, the ornate palace of the Umayyad sultans in Granada, stood out as engineering and esthetic marvels. The gardens, fountains, and other public works in the Muslim cities were renowned for their beauty and functionality. Islamic Spain, however, was also a constant reminder of the religious and cultural threat Islam posed to Christian European feudalism. The Muslim cities of Spain were, in short, both admired and feared by the enemies of Islam.

their labor and produce to those above them in exchange for defense and civil management. Military obligations formed a core component of the English system. Led by nobles, English peasants were expected to serve the common defense in militia-like units known as *fyrds*. Although the *fyrd* was a local force, its overall feudal characteristics were obvious: Military service was a duty owed, regardless of its impact on the individual called to it, and it was in no way optional. No free man could refuse to serve in a local *fyrd*. If he did, he would be punished. In terms of military service and land tenure, then, the age of feudalism had begun in England.

The Challenge of Islam

The barbarian kingdoms were maturing at a rapid pace by the time the Islamic prophet Muhammad claimed to have been selected as God's messenger. All over Europe, new models of social, political, and economic relations were being tried and tested. In the Middle East and North Africa, however, far older modes of organization prevailed. Persia clung to imperial forms that were reminiscent of the Roman Empire, while in Arabia clans held sway. Clan patriarchs rather than local nobles filled the leadership roles among the desert folk. Ultimate and often unchecked power resided in clan and family headmen. The religion Muhammad founded, Islam, therefore, was fundamentally tribal and absolutist in its outlook. The complexities that had already come to characterize early European feudalism did not exist in the Arabian order. So, in addition to being opposed to Christian thinking (Islam held that Jesus was merely a prophet and not the son of God), Islam represented a threat to feudal concepts of society and politics.

None of this would have mattered much had Islam not spread so quickly toward Europe. After Muhammad's death in 632 the geographic expansion of Islam was relentless. By the early eighth century Muslim armies had conquered all of the Middle East, taken North Africa, and pushed into Europe. Only military defeats in France (732) and at the gates of Constantinople (718) kept Islam from ending Europe's feudal experiment. Pushed back momentarily, Islam lingered on the outskirts of the European world, ready to move against it again at a later date. And yet, the victories over the forces of Islam left Europe secure and well prepared for the next stage in feudalism's history.

Chapter Two

Charlemagne to Clermont

History credits Charles Martel with the defeat of the Muslims in France. Charles Martel led the Frankish armies at the battle of Tours (732). Technically, his title was "mayor of the palace," meaning that he served the Frankish king as something like a chief assistant. In reality, Charles Martel operated almost as a coruler. It was he who defended not only France but also the entirety of western Europe from the invading Muslim warriors. It was also Charles Martel who began a line of kings famous for producing a man who would usher in the classical period of European feudalism—Charlemagne.

Charles Martel's son Pépin III did what his father never dared: He stole the crown of the Franks for himself. Pépin decided that being the power behind the throne, as Charles Martel had been, was not enough. He maneuvered himself into a position where the Frankish nobility agreed to make him king in 752. Know-ing that he had a weak claim to the monarchy, Pépin went out of his way to strengthen ties between the Frankish state and the church. Pépin also worked hard to reinforce and expand the role of the nobility in governing his realm. He gave many nobles important government offices and made them his personal advisers. Yet the details of consolidating his rule did not distract Pépin from the equally important task of producing an heir. Pépin and his wife had a son who was named after his grandfather.

Pépin III's son Charles grew up to be a fine, strong, tall young man. Intelligent and athletic, Charles loved to hunt and to play a variety of sports, the more physical and violent the better. He learned to ride a horse and use weapons, but he never mastered reading and writing. Charles tried to teach himself these skills, but he failed. According to one of Charles's friends, he "tried to write, and used to keep tablets and blanks under his

Charlemagne, emperor of the Holy Roman Empire, ushered in the classical period of European feudalism.

pillow, that at leisure hours he might accustom his hand to form the letters; however, as he did not begin his efforts in due season, but late in life, they met with ill success."[7] Pépin, of course, cared less about his son's academic studies than his training in the military arts. Young Charles would someday alter the history of Europe wielding a sword, not a pen.

The opportunity to make history came in 768. Pépin III died and left his crown to Charles. It was clear from the start that the new king would exceed his father's accomplishments. After assuming the throne Charles set out on a series of bold military campaigns to unite central Europe under his rule. He invaded Germany and subdued the Bavarians and Saxons. Then Charles, following up on a war begun by his father, attacked the Lombards in Italy and defeated them. Crushing the Lombards left the church in a position to become the political as well as religious master of Italy. The pope, not surprisingly, felt a deep sense of gratitude to Charles and invited him to Rome. He wanted to forge official links between the Church and the seemingly invincible Frankish king. In a deal that benefited both men, Pope Leo III, on Christmas Day in the year 800, crowned Charles as the emperor of a new empire, one that would later be known as the Holy Roman Empire. Charles took the name Charlemagne, or Charles the Great. As bells rang out and the choir sang, the people in the cathedral where the coronation took place voiced their hopes for the future. "Long life and victory to Charles Augustus, crowned by God, the great . . . emperor of the Romans!"[8] they exclaimed.

Duty and Obligation

Perhaps no European ruler left so indelible a mark on history as did Charlemagne. Certainly no one did more to accelerate the evolution of feudalism than he. To be sure, the age of feudalism began long before the Frankish monarch became the emperor. But Charlemagne's initiatives helped to formalize and spread the feudal system throughout Europe. Under Charlemagne, the king moved to the top of the feudal hierarchy in a way denied the earlier barbarian chieftains. Below him came the upper nobility and high church officials. The local nobility and clergy came next. Finally, the peasantry made its appearance, supporting the entire structure. At each level different duties and obligations applied.

Charlemagne's Palace School

Charlemagne regretted his near illiteracy every day of his life. Although he could read a little, the king could not write and therefore had no hope of attaining any success as a scholar, as did his English contemporary Alfred the Great. None of this, however, stopped Charlemagne from taking a keen interest in scholarship and education. In fact, the king compensated for his own academic shortcomings by establishing a palace school that quickly became famous for the quality of its teachers and curriculum. Charlemagne, determined to have around him an educated noble class, gathered together scholars from throughout his realm. These men he put to work studying and writing about a wide range of subjects. He also gave them the job of teaching Latin, literature, mathematics, and rhetoric to a select group of aristocratic boys. Charlemagne wanted to create a center of knowledge and inquiry at the palace school. The king also wanted to build a body of learning for the future, so he put one group of men to work copying, by hand, the important books of the day. To speed their job these scribes invented a new form of script known as Carolingian minuscule, or what we today call lower-case lettering.

Each person had responsibility for those below him and owed service to those above them. If the system were to function correctly, everyone would need to maintain their social position.

Land tied the entire system together. Charlemagne gave immense tracts of land to his closest followers, otherwise known as vassals, in exchange for their political loyalty and their availability for military service. Such a grant was called a *feudum*, and it conferred considerable authority and prestige upon the recipient. These men subsequently divided their land grants further, giving smaller parcels, or manors, to local nobles. The manors came with similar strings attached, namely loyalty and military obligation. These manors, or more precisely the fields attached to them, were worked by peasants who were bound to the land. They could neither leave it, nor could they refuse to work it. Serfs, as they were known, received both protection and the management of their community affairs from the manor lord in return. Serfs grew the food; nobles protected both the serfs and the food supply The king then united society under a single source of authority. For its part, the church gave God's approval to the entire system.

The Norse Migrations

When Charlemagne died in 814 he left behind the outline of an enduring feudal system. Set up as it was, Charlemagne's model provided for the two most basic requirements of life—food and defense. For this reason, it helped further the development of feudal insti-tutions throughout Europe. This could not have come at a better time, since the Vikings had begun to arrive on the coast of England in 793.

Known by scholars as the Norse, the Vikings (*i viking* means "the man who went plundering") were originally farmers and herders from Scandinavia. They often lived in inland towns and villages, but they maintained ancient connections to the sea. Fishing and sailing were commonplace to them, as were travel and communication by boat. The Vikings could be labeled, therefore, a sea people. They were also fierce warriors in search of a new home. Likely due to overcrowding and food shortages, compounded by climate change, the Vikings took to their longships just as Charlemagne was coming to power.

Sailing from what is now Denmark, Norway, and Sweden, the Vikings launched raids along the European coast and down the many rivers that penetrated deeply into Russia. Some of the raiding parties came and went, taking anything of immediate value with them. Most, however, were mere preludes to larger population movements. The pattern established among the majority of the Viking raiders was remarkably uniform: raids followed by migration and settlement. The Vikings, in other words, looted, but they also relocated entire communities in order to farm.

Contemporary accounts made much of the destruction caused by the Viking raids that began in England but soon spread along the coasts of Scotland, Ireland, and France. One churchman com-

A Viking warrior's helmet, most likely used during one of the many Viking raids along the European coast.

plained that no matter what local communities tried to do, the Vikings could not be stopped. "We pay them continually," the English archbishop Wulfstan lamented, "and they humiliate us daily; they ravage and they burn, plunder and rob."[9] Similar statements flowed from the pens of writers throughout western Europe who had contact with the Vikings, but only a few noted the Norse habit of settling down in the very places they terrorized. Those reports echoed the surprise of an observer who noted that after a raid the Vikings would "build themselves houses . . . as it [the place they attacked] were to be their permanent dwelling place."[10]

Feudalism's First Test

Given this tendency to combine war and peace, continental Europeans drew on the new system of feudalism to defend against the Norse invaders and, if that failed, absorb them into their communities. Many places exposed to Viking raids resisted them vigorously and often quite successfully. The localized nature of the feudal military system was well suited to oppose hit-and-run operations such as those favored by many Viking bands. Eminently flexible and always available, feudal defense networks could be relied upon to counter the Viking threat wherever it appeared. No doubt the initial strike on a particular location might come as a surprise, but once aroused, local forces could easily respond to any follow-up attacks.

The dictates of feudal military obligation ensured that everyone with a stake in communal defense, from duke to manor lord to peasant farmer, served in the military and remained on alert until the danger had passed. Moreover, because all command and control were local, these forces could move with astonishing speed to the points where they were most needed. Although on rare occasions it could prove amateurish, the feudal levy, as it was called, succeeded in putting armed men where they were required to deal with Viking raids. This guaranteed, according to some historians, that "Viking defeats were more numerous than victories."[11]

Even where the Vikings did prove successful, feudalism could still deny the Norse a permanent victory. Absorption was the case here. In those areas where the Vikings settled in large numbers, such as England and northern France, feudalism, if not completely mature, was already well established and functioned smoothly. It also represented an advance over Norse forms of community organization. Rather than replace it, then, the Vikings accepted feudalism. It helped that feudalism was based on a model familiar to many Norse people, in which independent nobles ruled over tenant farmers. This and other aspects of feudal European society made it easier for the Vikings to become absorbed in local communities. In England, for example, after an initial phase of hostility the Viking intruders merged seamlessly into Anglo-Saxon society even though an agreed-upon border, the Danelaw, separated the newcomers from their involuntary hosts.

Norse explorers land on the coast of France. Many places exposed to Norse invaders resisted them vigorously and often quite successfully.

A Case of Cultural Absorption— The Danelaw

Perhaps the most successful instance of cultural absorption during the age of feudalism began as an effort at ethnic segregation. In the year 878 the Anglo-Saxon king Alfred the Great soundly defeated a Norse army from Denmark that had invaded England. Unable to conquer the whole of the island, the Danes settled for part of it. They and Alfred reached an agreement to divide England between them. The Norse would take the area above a line drawn along the Thames River; the Anglo-Saxons would rule the area below it. This line, drawn by the antagonists, was known as the Danelaw, and it was supposed to separate the two peoples forever. In reality, the line, like all such arbitrary borders in history, actually brought people together. Traditions, customs, and especially language passed over and through the Danelaw as if it were a cultural highway. Anglo-Saxons and Norse traded, talked, and intermarried all along the frontier, creating a new blended culture that spread from the border northward and southward throughout England. An artificial divide, designed to isolate two groups, ended up combining them and producing an English heritage that was enriched by diversity.

By the middle of the tenth century the Norse were being integrated into societies and cultures that they had been assaulting just a century before. In some instances the Norse influence on local development simply evaporated, but in others the Viking presence created hybrid communities in which feudal institutions only grew stronger as the Norse settled down, married local people, and began farming in England.

The Magyar Menace

Feudalism also proved to be more than a match for another challenger, this one from the steppes of central Asia. Around the year 900 the Magyars, warrior nomads from the East, began migrating into the heart of Europe. With their ferocious horsemen in the vanguard, the Magyars rode over the Carpathian Mountains and penetrated Europe as far as southern Germany. Armed with powerful bows and fierce determination, the Magyars conquered vast areas of territory. Eventually, they consolidated their rule in the region of present-day Hungary. They were followed closely by waves of Slavic immigrants from Russia who exploited the opening made by the Magyars.

Numbering perhaps four hundred thousand, the Magyars represented the same degree of threat to central Europe as the Vikings did in western Europe. Local populations hated and feared them.

A priest who recorded their arrival wrote that the Magyars were "unaware of the all-powerful God, [but] not ignorant of every type of crime and murder and eager only for theft."[12] The Magyars were strong and ruthless but far from unstoppable. A feudal army raised by a German king utterly defeated them in 955, a blow from which they never recovered. After that, Magyar raids came to a halt. The people who had been the terror of eastern and central Europe fell back to their region of Hungary for protection. There they settled down and slowly adopted feudal political, social, and economic forms. Though there was somewhat less ethnic blending in the Magyar lands than in England, the same basic process of absorption took place. Soon there were Magyar nobles overseeing the labor of serfs within the framework of a system predicated upon landholding.

Church and State

The Viking and Magyar onslaught of the ninth and tenth centuries accelerated feudal evolution across Europe. During this period the feudal military model, in which one was obligated to give military service to the man from whom land was obtained, became highly formalized and almost universally adopted. Kings could now raise large armies very quickly, simply by invoking their vassals' obligation. Rulers even began to specify the precise manner in which a noble who "held his land of the king"[13] would fulfill his military obligation. Lords were to provide the king with infantry, often no more than armed peasants, and armored mounted knights. Knights, clad in various forms of armor and sitting atop huge horses, functioned as shock troops—soldiers whose job it was to win battles through the sheer strength of their attack—from the tenth century on. The nobility was also told to fortify its homes and territorial possessions. The resulting walled compounds later developed into full-fledged castles.

Military service was understood to be the legitimate price paid for security in the age of feudalism, but there were other ways to guarantee peace and stability. Christianity, in fact, was a very efficient tool for taming enemies of the state. Since the fifth century, church leaders and the political elite had been using religion to ensure conformity and reinforce their power. The once-mighty Magyars, for instance, had been so thoroughly converted to Christianity by the end of the tenth century that an observer at the time commented that the "people of the Hungarians [Magyars] who previously were accustomed cruelly to prey upon their neighbors, now freely give of their own for the sake of Christ. They who formerly pillaged the Christians . . . now welcome them like brothers and children."[14]

More than once, conversion to Christianity brought outsiders into the feudal fold. The details of the process were the same no matter where one happened to be. Invasion was followed by an initial period of violence, during which local institutions were disrupted. The instigators of the violence were met and defeated by military force. The defeated people settled down, began to assimilate, and were soon preached the word of God. The foreign elite converted, usually for political reasons, and were quickly imitated by the common folk. After aggressive preaching, the church gradually became involved in the daily affairs of the newly converted group. When a kingdom emerged that either included or was dominated by the assimilated people, the clergy took positions as key functionaries at all levels of administration. Law, diplomacy, and any other job requiring literacy and world knowledge, of which the medieval church had a virtual monopoly, often went to men associated with the church.

Conversion neutralized threats to the feudal order and further solidified the connection between church and state; bringing the clergy into government made that bond seem real. No one questioned the role of the state in promoting religion or religion in promoting the state. The relationship was taken for granted. Church and state operated as one. There were and would be serious conflicts and disputes between the two, but in terms of how people understood the feudal order of things, they were inseparable. Peasants looked up through the social and political hierarchy and saw not only nobles and kings but also bishops and popes.

Islam—Again

It would have been a rare case for one of these tenant farmers, serfs, or local craftspeople to have known much, if anything

Christ's Church Divided

Early Christianity had represented a single body of faith. There had always been disputes and differences, but the basic contours of the religion had been universally accepted by its followers. Yet as Christianity grew, two distinct lineages emerged, one Latin and the other Greek. One of these lines could be traced to Rome, the other to Byzantium (Constantinople after 330). Over time, two Christian traditions appeared in the western and eastern parts of the Roman Empire. When the empire split at the end of the fourth century, so did the church. Officially, Christianity remained one religion, but in practice one half looked for guidance to the bishop of Rome, while the other united under the leadership of the patriarch of Constantinople. The collapse of the empire highlighted this split and exacerbated religious and cultural tensions that had been worsening for centuries. Over the next six hundred years eastern and western Christianity drifted ever farther apart. As time passed, they had less in common and more in dispute. In 1054 an argument over how to respond to the occupation of southern Italy by the Normans, French descendents of Norse invaders, resulted in a final divorce between the Latin and Eastern Orthodox churches.

A crusader, a Christian soldier, fights a Muslim soldier. Christians saw Islam as a threat to political, social, and religious institutions.

at all, about Islam. Unless one lived in a place like Spain, where daily contact and interaction between Muslims and Christians were common beginning in the eighth century, Muslims were a distant and alien people. The elite, however, knew of and feared the followers of Muhammad, and by the eleventh century Islam was rising again to threaten them. Since Charlemagne's accession, kings and popes, church and state had become almost indistinguishable. What affected one affected the other. Thus, when Islam threatened Europe once again, it threatened a web of political, social, and religious institutions.

The Muslims, of course, did not know this; they had their own agenda. For nearly three hundred years Islam and Christianity had been at war along the fringes of the Byzantine Empire. What the Muslims sought was unchallenged control over the eastern Mediterranean Sea. The Byzantine Empire stood in their way. In 1071 a Muslim army defeated the Byzantines at the battle of Manzikert and seemed poised to overrun the empire. Although feudalism had not taken root in the Byzantine world, and the eastern and western Christian churches had been separate entities since 1054, the Muslim victory at Manzikert alarmed the European elite. They worried that the continent might be next, and this time there might not be a Charles Martel to save it. The church, the monarchs, and the nobility feared for their survival.

But this was not the Europe of the barbarian kingdoms any longer. After hundreds of years fighting off invaders and building the feudal system, Europe was unwilling to tolerate yet another challenge from Islam. Fearful but nonetheless defiant, Christian feudal Europe decided to strike first, an intention it made clear at a place called Clermont.

Chapter Three

The Church Militant

Pope Urban II arrived at Clermont, in France, determined to respond to what he saw as a clear danger to Christianity and the European way of life. He called for an assembly to discuss what to do about Islam. The leading nobles of France were assembled before the pope that day in 1095; the warrior-kings and nobility of England, Germany, and Spain would learn of the meeting later. Urban opened the meeting by recounting how in the seventh century the Muslims had charged in and taken the Holy Land (ancient Palestine), the very birthplace of Jesus Christ. He then went on to summarize Islam's expansion since that date and its unrelenting assault on the Byzantine Empire. The pope charged the Muslims with having "violently invaded the lands of those Christians and . . . depopulated them by pillage and fire."[15]

The French nobles listened politely to Urban's history lesson and waited patiently for him to get to the point. Then, as if on cue, it came. The pope claimed that Muslims were butchering Christian women and children. Churches, he charged, had been desecrated and turned into mosques. The land of Jesus was in the hands of infidels, or nonbelievers. Urban spat out one vile accusation after another, until he paused dramatically and asked, "On whom, therefore, rests the labor of avenging these wrongs and of recovering this territory, if not you?"[16] The assembly waited only a moment before crying out, "It is the will of God! It is the will of God!"[17] With that, the feudal war machine was set into motion to reassert Christian control of Palestine and safeguard the European social model. The First Crusade had begun.

Knights and Holy War

The eleventh and twelfth centuries witnessed the rise of the armored knight to a place of legendary prominence. Knights, in essence mounted nobles

Pope Urban II proposes the First Crusade at an assembly in Clermont, France.

wearing some form of armor, had been around since the days of the Roman Empire. There they had been known as *equites* and constituted a part of Rome's political elite. Armored barbarian warriors on horseback had similarly represented the military and political elite of their day. The Byzantines likewise had horsemen, covered in chain mail and later plate steel, specialized troops they called cataphracts, who occupied a unique place in eastern imperial society. Yet the feudal knight was a different sort of military, social, and cultural creation.

The knights that Urban II inspired to defend Christendom had been elevated to a position unheard of in previous times and places. Much more than noble soldiers, they were the axis upon which feudalism turned. One might be higher or lower on the social ladder, but the knight is where it all started. The knight, moreover, fulfilled some of the weightiest responsibilities in society. A twelfth-century English philosopher described the knight's duties, among many others, as being to "protect the Church . . . to fend off injustice from the poor . . . to shed blood for brethren, and if needs must, to lay down [his] life."[18] Knights were understood to be holy warriors, social avengers, and loyal comrades. They faithfully served their superiors and protected those below them. Obligation, duty, and responsibility were a knight's motto. The knight was the true example of the feudal order.

In more literal terms, however, the knight was a lesser noble, often possessing little more of value than his title. Few knights could claim much in the way of real wealth. Each owed service to his immediate lord and, through him, to the king (his liege lord, as he was called). In return for some land and the rights to the food grown on it, the knight was to provide forty days of mounted military service per year. His horse and all other equipment were purchased at his own expense.

Chivalry, the code of conduct that became the hallmark of knighthood, was just coming into existence in the eleventh and twelfth centuries. Although chivalry is most often associated with helping damsels in distress, it really had more to do with how knights would kill in battle. For all its talk of aiding the weak and defenseless, as the historian John A. Lynn has noted, "chivalry was ultimately about violence."[19] Knights were first and foremost soldiers. Now, in 1095, the pope was asking them to fight and kill for God. At other points in time men might have declined such a request, but in the age of feudalism duty was duty, especially to the church. God was everyone's lord. War, more so when it was called holy, was a knight's job.

The Peasantry

Underneath the popes, kings, lords, bishops, and knights were the common folk—the peasantry. Either as tenant farmers who paid rent on their farms or as serfs who labored out of feudal obligation, the peasants were bound to the land and the noblemen who held it. Unlike anyone else in feudal society, peasants literally earned their living from their labor. They were the base of society,

Serfs, who often lived in extreme poverty, labored out of feudal obligation to the noblemen who owned the land.

the agrarian workforce that grew the wheat, rye, and barley that fed Europe. Unable to leave the soil they tilled, peasants were often exploited and occasionally brutalized by the people above them. They lived in extreme poverty and usually were not able to escape. Peasants experienced disease and died from it at higher levels than anyone else in society. Dependent upon the fields they worked for food, a poor crop year meant long periods of hunger for peasant families.

Looked down upon by their masters, peasants were nonetheless crucial to the feudal system. Nobles of all degrees, from duke to humble knight, relied upon the strong backs and hardworking hands of peasants to make the land flourish.

Bountiful harvests made the nobility wealthy and powerful, but peasants made the harvests bountiful. The church, perhaps Europe's single largest landlord, similarly depended upon the peasantry. The clergy took not only its share of the food grown by peasants but also drew on them for legitimacy. The church was only as strong as its followers' faith and devotion. Masses attended by loyal Christians were the church's ultimate source of power. If the peasantry ever doubted the clergy or withdrew its support, as would happen in the sixteenth century, the church's position in society would be in jeopardy. The church, in short, needed both the peasants' labor and their faithfulness.

The Pope's Knights

Combining two of the age of feudalism's defining institutions, the clergy and the knighthood, the religious orders of the Knights Templar, Hospitaler, and Teutonic embodied the fervor of the crusades. The Teutonic Knights, formed in Germany in 1190, fought for the church in the Holy Land and later in eastern Europe. Clad in white tunics bearing a black cross, the Teutonic Knights attained legendary status in Germany, giving inspiration to future German writers, artists, and philosophers. The Knights of St. John of Jerusalem originated as an order devoted to caring for sick pilgrims, hence the name Hopitalers. Wearing their trademark white cross on black tunics, the Knights of St. John zealously defended the church and won wide renown for their exploits on the battlefield. The Templars (the Knights of the Temple) took their name from the location of their headquarters in Jerusalem on the site where King Solomon's temple in ancient times was reputed to have been. Bearing a red cross on white, the Templars participated in every major engagement fought in Palestine. Regardless of their origins or insignia, the religious knightly orders were respected, feared, and hated by their opponents.

Feudal Europe could be imagined as a society in balance. As the scholar Georges Duby noted, peasants balanced out the influence of the clergy and nobility. "On one side," he wrote in his study of the medieval economy, "was placed the non-producers, monks, clerks, men of war; on the other . . . the workers . . . the peasants."[20] Peasants grew food, constructed buildings, dug ditches, paved roads, cut wood, and quarried stones for Europe's castles and cathedrals. Those for whom they labored were anything but grateful. The peasantry, however, expected as much; they were used to sacrificing themselves. They took for granted struggle and suffering in both war and peace.

Wars were begun by nobles and churchmen, and they were supposedly fought by knights. Yet many peasants, at least those such as tenant farmers who were considered free men, found themselves called up for service with their lords. Even when not fighting, peasants bore the burden of providing war supplies and enduring the consequences of warfare in an age before organized national armies. In between formal battles, ill-disciplined knights wandered around the countryside terrorizing the peasantry. Their adventures included theft, physical abuse, and disruption of farm work. Villages were robbed; grain was stolen; farmers were assaulted and on occasion killed. Feudal armies, especially those far from home in the service of the king, routinely wreaked havoc on local communities. When Urban called for a crusade to liberate the Holy Land, Europe's

peasants knew that their hard lot was about to become harder.

The Drive to Jerusalem

Muslim armies had conquered Jerusalem in 638. At Clermont, over four hundred years later, the Christians announced their intention to get it back. The pope took care of arousing the passions of Europe's nobles and convincing them to take up the cross. The local clergy performed the same feat on local manors and in towns and villages far removed from the centers of political and religious power. Fired by religious zeal, peasants as well as knights answered the call of service. They paid a heavy price for it.

Even before the nobility took up the knight's sword itself for war with Islam, a peasant "army" set out for Jerusalem. Inflamed by the ranting of an insane monk named Peter the Hermit, who claimed to be guided by visions from God, tens of thousands of French and German peasants, "more numerous than the sands of the sea,"[21] it was reported, made their way from central Europe to Constantinople. Mostly unarmed, few if any of these people knew what they were supposed to do when they met the Muslims. They did not have to wonder very long. Peter's "army" was massacred by a force of Muslim Turks just outside the Byzantine capital.

More serious and better-conceived efforts followed Peter the Hermit's tragic fiasco. Nobles, in the early days mainly from France, activated the feudal obligation system and marshaled their forces. Knights gathered together to set out for

The vicious battle between the crusaders and the Muslims in 1099, where thousands of Muslims were massacred.

French nobleman Godfrey of Bouillon, who captured Jerusalem in 1099 during the First Crusade.

the Holy Land. They were promised gifts of land and riches in return for fighting on behalf of Christendom. Military service was often sweetened in this manner. Land meant wealth and perhaps an opportunity for advancement upward through the ranks of nobility. The crusaders were also given something called "plenary indulgence" by the pope himself. This meant that whatever horrible acts the crusaders committed against the Muslims, civilian and soldier alike, would not count as sins against their Christian souls. In essence, the pope, acting as God's representative on earth, was able to forgive rape, torture, and murder if they were being committed in God's name.

With clear consciences and sharp words, the newly recruited crusaders left in 1096. They were forbidden to harm any Christian peasants or townsfolk along the way. This so-called Peace of God did not, however, apply to Jews. They were harassed, robbed, beaten, and killed by crusaders who viewed them as enemies of Christ and a blight on Europe. While Jews, who denied that Jesus was the son of God, were considered fair game, in practice even Christian peasants fell victim to the crusaders' stealing, torture, and other horrendous behavior. Even though the Peace of God was supposed to protect Christians, most crusaders paid little heed to calls for restraint. Restrictions on who could be abused seemingly applied only if one got caught. Crusaders on the move were a law unto themselves.

Thus, the Christian army pressed eastward. Led by two Frankish nobles, God-frey of Bouillon and Raymond of Saint-Gilles, the crusaders captured Antioch, the first city they came to in the Holy Land. After an eight-month siege, the city fell in June 1098. From there the warriors marched southward to Jerusalem. Over the course of the next year they fought one Muslim force after another, large and small. Meanwhile, Jerusalem's elders, well aware of the Europeans' approach, slammed shut the gates, hoping that the high, thick walls around them would keep the Christians out.

Their hopes were misplaced. Godfrey and Raymond arrived on June 7, 1099. Using huge siege towers, battering rams, and scaling ladders, all constructed on the spot, the crusaders pounded away at Jerusalem's defenses. They breeched the city's walls in just over a month and stormed the city. What followed was one of history's most infamous massacres. The church had stoked the fires of religious and ethnic hatred for four years. From pope to local priest, churchmen had urged the Christian nobility to retake the Holy City and avenge the Muslim insult to God. The Muslims, it was said, were the tools of Satan. No mercy could be shown to them.

Enraged and confident that they were doing the Lord's work, the crusaders rampaged through the streets of Jerusalem. An ancient place, sacred to Christianity, Judaism, and Islam alike, Jerusalem suffered. Its streets echoed with the screams of innocent people cut down by Christian swords. One knight remembered that "the slaughter was so great that our men waded in blood up to their ankles."[22] A priest who followed the crusaders into the city justified the murder of nearly every Muslim and Jew living there by saying, "It was a just and splendid judgment of God that the place should be filled with the blood of unbelievers."[23] Exhausted from the butchering, the crusaders piled forty thousand bodies outside of Jerusalem's gates when they had finished. The killers then went to church to thank God for their triumph.

The Second Crusade

The church had met with perhaps its greatest political and military success the day Jerusalem fell. Still, total victory eluded the Christians. True, the territory conquered by the invading Europeans was quickly fortified and organized into four crusader states, actually miniature kingdoms—the County of Edessa, the County of Tripoli, the Principality of Antioch, and the Kingdom of Jerusalem—but the Muslim presence was far from erased. Beyond the borders of the crusader states, the regrouped armies of Islam were poised to counterattack. The European foothold in the Middle East would not be secure until Islam was crushed.

Recognizing this fact, the church moved aggressively once again. In 1146 Bernard of Clairvaux, a clergyman who would one day be declared a saint, preached another crusade. Encouraged by the pope, Bernard toured France, speaking at length about the recent and shocking conquest of the County of Edessa by a Muslim force led by the new sultan, Imad al-Din Zengi. Bernard told his noble audiences that this fresh outrage was an affront to God, and God demanded their services once more. He proved to be a very persuasive speaker. "I opened my mouth," Bernard boasted in a letter to the pope, "I spoke and at once the Crusaders have multiplied to infinity."[24] The feudal nobility took up its sword for a second time.

The events that followed seemed like those taken from a tragic comedy. A crusader army led by Conrad of Germany, Louis VII of France (St. Louis), and Baldwin III, king of Jerusalem, marched for the Muslim capital of Damascus in Syria. Misfortune struck from the very beginning of the expedition. The German contingent never even reached Syria; the Muslims destroyed the group at its staging area in Palestine. The Franks and their comrades from Jerusalem experienced supply problems and disputes over the chain of command. Pulling themselves together, the force from Jerusalem finally made it to the outskirts of Damascus mid-year in 1148 and laid siege to the city. The Muslim troops easily held out long enough for disagreements among their enemies to resurface and multiply. Eventually, the crusader army fell apart of its own accord and retreated home in disgrace. The church militant had to endure the sting of its first defeat.

Saladin and the Muslim Reconquest

The failure of the Second Crusade marked the turning of the tide in Palestine. The debacle in Syria provided an

Bernard of Clairvaux, a clergyman who later was declared a saint, preached for a second crusade.

Saladin, the Sultan of Islam

Saladin was born into conflict and turmoil. His mother died when he was young, and his father was forever surrounded by political controversy. In fact, just after Saladin's birth in the now-Iraqi city of Tikrit in 1137, his father and uncle Shirkuh were forced to flee their hometown and settle in territory governed by a powerful Muslim warlord, an old acquaintance and future sultan named Imad al-Din Zengi. There, Saladin was raised by his father, although he was educated in the military arts by his uncle. When his father moved to Damascus in the service of Imad al-Din's son and successor, Saladin dutifully followed and began a career as one of the new sultan's most trusted lieutenants. Later, he used his position as a springboard to take power for himself after a ferocious civil war against Imad al-Din's grandsons. Saladin, as sultan, became famous for uniting Syria and Egypt into a single Muslim state and using its might to retake the holy city of Jerusalem in 1187. During the crusades he gained a reputation as a fierce warrior who was nevertheless a compassionate and faithful Muslim. After his death in 1193 he was eulogized as "the ornament and admiration of the world," as cited in John Davenport's *Saladin*.

Quoted in John Davenport, *Saladin*. Philadelphia: Chelsea House, 2003, p. 100.

Saladin, the sultan of Islam, commanded Muslim forces in the Third Crusade.

opening for the Muslims, if they could exploit it. The desire to crush the crusader states and regain Jerusalem had simmered since 1099, but disunity and the absence of a competent and charismatic leader doomed any attempt to do more than keep the Christians on the defensive. Now, it was the Europeans who were in disarray and vulnerable. The right man in the right place could turn Christian confusion into Muslim victory.

Such a figure emerged in the person of Salah al-din Yusuf Ibn Ayyub—Saladin. A Kurdish Muslim born in Tikrit (in modern-day Iraq) in 1137, Saladin rose to become sultan in 1184 through a combination of political intrigue and outright civil war. His self-appointed mission since boyhood had been the expulsion of the Christians from all of the Holy Land. To this end, Saladin collected a mighty army that included warriors from throughout the Muslim world and prepared for war.

Saladin struck in June 1187. His target was Jerusalem. Slicing his way toward the heart of the crusader states, Saladin was met by a combined European army in the open desert at a place called Hattin. The Muslim commander promptly annihilated it and proceeded to recapture one city after another for Islam. Saladin finally took his prize on October 2, 1187. In a demonstration of incredible restraint, Saladin allowed the Christian defenders of Jerusalem to leave the city unharmed after paying a modest tribute to him. Celebrating Saladin's victory and his generosity, a Muslim cleric praised him as "the champion and protector of thy holy land, the great helping prince who gave might to the declaration of faith, who vanquished the adorers of the Cross . . . the Sultan of Islam."[25]

Boiling with rage upon receiving news of the Muslim triumph, Pope Clement III drew yet again upon the obligation of Europe's kings and nobles. He called for a Third Crusade. The response this time was overwhelming. Eager and determined knights clamored for a chance to go to Palestine and fight Saladin. An army commanded by the famous English king Richard the Lionhearted sailed for the Holy Land with a full complement of armored noblemen. Richard and his army arrived in June 1191 and promptly set to work against the Muslims. In a series of running battles, Richard bested Saladin. The English monarch captured the city of Acre, defeated the Muslims at Arsuf, and occupied the city of Ashqelon after Saladin had destroyed everything of value to keep it from falling into Christian hands. The crusaders were winning, but Richard had exhausted himself and his men during the course of his Palestine campaign. He requested a meeting with Saladin in 1192. The result was a truce that left Jerusalem, in fact all of the Holy Land, to the Muslims in return for a guarantee of Christian access to religious sites. Saladin died the very next year, having ended the European adventure in the Middle East. Richard followed his old enemy in death in 1199.

Bloodlust, Folly, and the Last Crusades

The church organized five more crusades before they realized its military could no longer fight. Each crusade was more fu-

Richard the Lionhearted, king of England, commanded English troops during the Third Crusade.

tile and ridiculous than the last. The sheer brutality of some of them shocked even the most devout and dutiful supporters of the church's crusading program. In 1204 a crusading army sacked Constantinople, gleefully slaughtering fellow Christians. Four years later other crusaders massacred religious dissenters in France. Men, women, and children, whose only crime was to urge a program to reform the church, were cut down in cold blood by men serving the pope. The church, frustrated by the Muslims, turned its fury on it own people. Perhaps the most horrible of the last crusades took place in 1212. Known as the Children's Crusade, an army of young children made an absurd attempt to reconquer the Holy Land. Armed with nothing more than an immature understanding of feudal duties to church and state, the children made their way to ports in the south of France only to be kidnapped and sold into slavery.

After the Children's Crusade, four more efforts to expand the boundaries of

The Horns of Hattin

Perhaps Saladin's greatest victory, and the one that opened the road to Jerusalem, took place near the Horns of Hattin. The battle pitted the sultan against his two most dangerous and determined Christian adversaries—Guy, king of Jerusalem, and Reginald of Châtillon. Guy rightfully feared that Saladin would make good on his threat to recapture the holy city, while Reginald was simply a pathological Muslim-hater. Both men, for their own reasons, welcomed a showdown with the sultan. Their plan was to march out of Jerusalem and meet him in open battle long before he could reach the city. Saladin, by far the better strategist, anticipated such a course of action and deftly played to its inherent weaknesses. The sultan knew that leaving Jerusalem meant that the Christian soldiers would also be leaving their sources of water, so he purposely lured Guy and Reginald onto the desolate plain of Hattin between the twin peaks known as the Horns. By the time the crusaders realized their mistake, they were dying of thirst and surrounded by the Muslim army. Their defeat was total. The Christian army was destroyed and its commanders captured. Saladin executed Reginald but freed Guy, graciously explaining, as cited in James Reston Jr.'s *Warriors of God: Richard the Lionheart and Saladin in the Third Crusade,* that "Real kings do not kill each other."

Quoted in James Reston Jr., *Warriors of God: Richard the Lionheart and Saladin in the Third Crusade.* New York: Doubleday, 2001, p. 56.

During the Children's Crusade an army of young children made an attempt to reconquer the Holy Land. They failed and were kidnapped and sold into slavery.

European Christianity came to nothing. Some ended in humiliation, others in total disaster. Regardless of the outcome, it was clear that the militancy of the church had burned itself out. The system of feudal obligation that had protected Europe against waves of invaders failed on the offensive just as it had succeeded on the defensive. What had worked against Vikings and Magyars failed miserably when confronted by Islam. The crusades pushed feudal Europe to its physical and psychological limits, leaving it unprepared to combat a new and much more lethal, albeit invisible, enemy.

Chapter Four

The Black Death

Europe was utterly exhausted after nearly two hundred years of war. The failure to defeat Islam left it weakened in faith as well. The reputation of the nobility had been damaged, in some ways beyond repair. The Christian warrior elite had proven itself useless against its Muslim counterpart. The Islamic cry of "God is great!" still rang out over the Holy Land. The supposedly all-powerful church had battled the enemies of Jesus—and lost. Even the relatively simple task of reuniting the eastern and western versions of Christianity had been beyond Rome's ability. Despite the exertions of the pope, the Eastern Orthodox Church continued to minister to the needs of Byzantine souls. After the crusades, popular confidence in the twin pillars of feudalism—the nobility and the church—had been shaken to its foundation.

The crisis in faith, bad as it was by the end of the thirteenth century, only grew worse over the next few decades. All the news seemed to be some troubling event or another. Violence and disorder gripped the continent. England and France, perhaps the two greatest feudal kingdoms in Europe, went to war with each other in 1346. They would continue the struggle for over a century. The pope, increasingly at odds with the Italian nobility, moved the capital of the church from Rome to the French city of Avignon, abandoning a place that had been the center of the Christian world for a millennium. The church and state bond began to strain. German armies under the command of Holy Roman emperor Henry VII invaded Italy, prompting the outbreak of civil war on the peninsula. Food shortages became commonplace; everywhere the crime rate soared. Feudal estates, so long the source of answers, now generated only questions and a creeping sense of uncertainty. How long the system itself would last no one knew.

Everyday Life in the Fourteenth Century

People responded to the growing chaos by trying to maintain an air of confident normality. Business as usual offered a thread of hope at a time when life was threatening to unravel. The manor, manse, demesne, whatever it was called in different parts of Europe, endured as the anchor of social and economic activity. The manor lord, as was his feudal duty, continued to oversee the cultivation of food and the organization of labor. He did so either personally or through his many village-level representatives, such as the bailiff, beadle, and reeve. The manor lord still provided security and mediated disputes through the manor court, just as he had always done. His serfs and tenant farmers repaid the lord with due subordination and service. They obeyed the manor lord, worked the land, and strove to keep village life harmonious and productive.

Living according to time-honored traditions helped Europeans feel better and more secure, but they still welcomed change. One of these changes was urbanization. "Town air makes men free,"[26] it was said, and towns and cities in the early fourteenth century were thriving as they had not done since the days of the ancient empire. London exploded to 30,000 inhabitants. Paris counted over 100,000 residents. In 1300 the Italian city of Milan had a population of 150,000. And these cities buzzed with economic activity. Large- and small-scale manufacturing expanded at a dizzying pace. Weaving, glassmaking, leatherwork, and

paint production were but a few of the hundreds of industries that sprang up in cities across Europe. Along with factories, foundries, and mills came skilled workers who organized themselves through craft guilds. The guilds were essentially craft-specific organizations that regulated prices and set standards of workmanship. In this way they helped bring a measure of order to urban economic life. Urban government likewise became more sophisticated and intrusive. Municipal governments extended their authority in many areas, including trade, civil law, and public works. The practice of electing local leaders became widespread, and popular oversight of elected officials became accepted practice in many places.

Whereas feudal institutions were being reenergized on the manor, they were being discarded in the cities. In important respects, feudalism was being eclipsed at the same time that it was reaching its peak of development. The irony of fourteenth-century feudalism continued in terms of trade and commerce. Coastal and river cities became home to merchant communities that operated independently. Partnering with political leaders, prosperous merchants competed to bring lucrative import-export businesses to their cities. Germany saw the advent of the Hanseatic League, a confederation of commercial towns that managed trade between northern Europe and Russia. England and Flanders pooled their efforts and came to dominate the wool cloth market. Italian city-states such as Venice and

Trade and commerce grew increasingly more important in Europe. Coastal and river cities became home to merchant communities that operated independently.

The Flagellants and the Plague

The tradition of wandering preachers, or mendicants, had deep roots in European Christianity. The idea was that by traveling the countryside in a perpetual state of self-denial, the mendicant helped Christians to recognize and atone for their sins. In the twelfth century this practice took a bizarre turn with the appearance of flagellants, people who walked the roads whipping themselves in repentance for their sins until their flesh was raw. According to *The Middle Ages* by Morris Bishop, a Franciscan friar who witnessed one such event noted that nobles and commoners alike "scourged themselves naked in procession through the cities, with the bishops and men of religion at their head." Although this strange practice fell out of favor rather quickly, it was revived during the Black Death. Wearing a white gown as a symbol of purity and as a means to showcase the blood to be shed, people took to the highways with whips in their hands once again during the epidemic of the fourteenth century. Flagellants became a common sight once more as men and women convinced themselves that sin had brought the curse of disease upon them. Initially tolerated by the Church hierarchy, the flagellants were suppressed when they drifted from repentance into heresy by linking physical torment directly to salvation.

Quoted in Morris Bishop, *The Middle Ages.* Boston: Houghton Mifflin, 1968, p. 171.

Genoa began to prosper as never before after they tapped into the trade routes from Asia. Acting as crucial middlemen, the Italian city-states acted as points of entry for spices, silk, porcelain, and other goods coming from India and China.

Whether through tradition or change, Europeans sought refuge in feudalism. Either by holding to its assumptions, as on the manor, or by moving beyond it, as in the cities, people still used feudalism as the reference point for their lives. Europeans could not ignore the outcome of the crusades nor could they miss the political conflict and tension that surrounded them. But so far nothing had happened to make them abandon the entire set of feudal relations that had been developed so painstakingly since the fall of Rome. Nothing yet had occurred that would force a search for a completely new social, political, and economic model.

The Plague

In late 1347 a ship arrived in Sicily from the port of Tana in the Crimea. It was a very nearly a ghost ship; most of its passengers and crew were dead or dying. When port officials boarded the eerily silent vessel, they found disfigured, stinking corpses, an obvious indication of disease. The officials promptly ordered the ship towed out of the harbor to keep whatever pestilence it carried isolated on board, but they were already too late. Some rats had scampered off onto the nearby streets of Messina. These runaway rats were carrying fleas, which in turn carried bacteria that caused a disease known as the plague.

Scientifically speaking, the unwanted and deadly new immigrant to Europe was *Yersinia pestis*, a bacterium that causes a devastating disease that came to be called the Black Death. Transported in the digestive systems of fleas, the illness had traveled from China, across Central Asia, to Europe. It arrived just as Europe was trying to recover not only from the social and psychological shock of the failed crusades but also in the wake of a famine that had struck between 1315 and 1317. Moreover, a climatic phenomenon called the Little Ice Age had begun to make temperatures cooler, making people more susceptible to acute illnesses.

Cold, hungry, weak, and emotionally worn out, Europe's population was unprepared to resist a vicious microscopic foe like *Y. pestis*; even less so when it is considered that the Black Death was really a composite term for three closely related disease forms. The most common was the bubonic plague. The fourteenth-century Italian writer Giovanni Boccaccio perhaps best described its painful and almost invariably fatal course:

> It began in both men and women with certain swellings in the groin or under the armpit. They grew in size to a small apple or egg, more or

The bubonic plague, also known as the Black Death, was a devastating illness, marking people with black spots that signaled imminent death.

less, and were vulgarly [commonly] called tumors. In a short span of time the tumors spread from the two parts named all over the body. Soon after then the symptoms changed and black and purple spots appeared on the arms and thighs. . . . These spots were a certain sign of death. . . . So violent was the malignancy of this plague that it was communicated, not only from one man to another, but from the garments of the sick.[27]

According to Boccaccio, even to "go near the sick brought the infection and common death to the living."[28] Marked for imminent demise by the unmistakable black spots, or buboes, people anticipated suffering gruesome ends.

Slightly less common but no less deadly were the other two types of plague, septicemic and pneumonic. Septicemic plague infected the blood and caused massive hemorrhaging and extreme pain. The pneumonic form caused inflammation of the lungs, intense chest pain, racking coughs, and spitting up of blood and lung tissue. In all these cases death came quickly, usually in a matter of days, but not before the infected person had suffered indescribable torment—and passed the disease on to other people.

The plague, as it appeared in Europe, was not only devastating but also well equipped to trigger an epidemic. Highly contagious, the Black Death thrived in the conditions it met. Poor nutrition and hygiene; human immune systems weakened by cold, hunger, and emotional stress;

large populations crowded into cities and towns; all this, compounded by rudimentary medical knowledge, established the perfect environment for the disease. Death, on a mass scale, was inevitable.

A Continent Infected

The ship that brought this terrifying disease to Europe was Genoese. Its dead and dying passengers had contracted bubonic plague while at a trading station in Central Asia. They had been infected during an attack on the outpost. The besiegers, local folk known as Tartars, had hurled bodies of plague victims over the station's walls in an attempt to terrify the defenders and perhaps spread the disease to them. The incident constituted the world's first recorded instance of biological warfare. Horrified at the sight of the disease-ravaged corpses tossed in their midst, the Genoese merchants fled for home, bringing the lethal bacterium with them.

Other Europeans, however, must have been infected around the same time, because the plague struck almost simultaneously at Constantinople, Marseilles, and the island of Sardinia; but Sicily proved to be the primary source of the contagion that raced up the Italian peninsula and then into the heart of the continent. By 1348, only one year after its arrival, the plague had spread throughout Italy, leaving perhaps 50 to 60 percent of its people dead. From there the Black Death crossed the Alps and dispersed in every direction. Austria, Hungary, and Germany were next. These places lost 30 to 40 percent of their populations. Soon

France was suffering. Half of its population died from the disease. In England the death toll climbed to 30 percent only months after the bacterium appeared there. Indeed, within a mere two years an estimated 25 million Europeans had perished. By 1351 no part of Europe remained untouched by the epidemic. Scandinavia and Russia saw death claim over 60 percent of their populations. Even the far Balkans experienced the catastrophe. So many people died there that it was rumored that "wolves . . . gloried in the unexpected windfall of fresh meat."[29] Scavenging animals and birds made a feast on the bodies of the dead.

War and famine, both of which struck at the same time as the plague, compounded the destruction. As people in England and France became ill and died, armies of the two kingdoms tore at the countryside during the Hundred Years' War. Battles and banditry swept over the peasantry and amplified the effects of disease. People would remember the famous military engagements of the long conflict between the English and the French, such as Crécy (1346) and Poitiers (1356), and often speak of the exploits of knights and kings, but few would recall the impact of war on the common folk. Already decimated by the Black Death, serfs and tenant farmers on both sides of the English Channel lived in fear of lawless soldiers, both the enemy's and their own. Battles, usually fought on open

Disease prevented workers from farming, leading to widespread famine. Soldiers often looted towns and confiscated what little food remained from those too ill to fight back.

farm fields, destroyed crops and left the ground unsuitable for tilling. Nearby villages were raided and grain stolen to feed the combatants. Worse still, roving bands of discharged men and deserters terrorized the peasants. Wherever men fought, local peasants suffered greatly.

Warriors pillaged and looted at a time of rampant crop failure. Insect infestations, plant blight, drought, torrential rain, or some combination of them ruined the grain harvests. Disease prevented the workforce from farming. Now, soldiers confiscated what little food remained. The result was widespread famine. Hunger gnawed at people's stomachs. Starvation set in, allowing diseases to spread even faster. The weakened peasants were unable to fend off both the bacterial and the human invaders. Conservative estimates put the overall European death rate by the end of the fourteenth century from war, famine, and plague at 50 percent or more of the total population. An equivalent rate in twenty-first century America would be over 150 million dead. Europe was devastated.

In Disaster's Wake

Europe could not absorb three successive blows to its population at once. The mortality rate was simply too high. The disruption of agricultural life and society was too great. Feudal Europe's population crashed. However, immediate death from warfare, starvation, and disease was only one factor. Dead, sick, or terrorized peasants could not farm. Throughout Europe, fields fell into dis-

use and remained this way for years on end. Grain supplies dwindled. In the short term this perpetuated the vicious cycle of hunger, weakness, disease, and more death. Stripped of its laborers, the land could not produce the grain that was the staple of the European diet. This led to malnutrition, famine, and a further decline in the laboring population. Less work meant less food and the downward spiral continued.

Long term, the consequences of what writer Barbara Tuchman once called "the calamitous fourteenth century"[30] were even more significant. Fear of illness and death deepened as the years passed, eventually being transformed into a pervasive sense of impending doom. Despair became chronic. A general feeling of hopelessness, an indescribable uneasiness, spread like a dark cloud over Europe. Some people soothed their pain by blaming vulnerable social minority groups, namely Jews. Jews across Europe were viewed as scapegoats, or the reason, for the epidemic. "In the matter of this plague," one fourteenth-century observer wrote, "the Jews . . . were reviled and accused in all lands of having caused it through the poison they were said to have put into the water and the wells . . . for this reason the Jews were burnt all the way from the Mediterranean to Germany."[31] Others became convinced that God had abandoned them and laid the blame for their misfortune not on Jews but on the church and the nobility. The men of God and the men of the sword had failed them. The elite were supposed to be blessed by the Lord, but they were

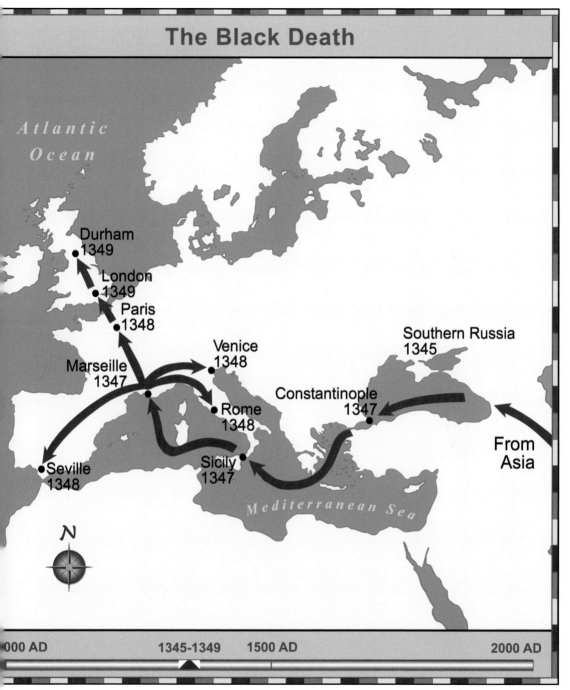

The Black Death

Durham
1349

London
1349

Paris
1348

Marseille
1347

Venice
1348

Rome
1348

Seville
1348

Sicily
1347

Constantinople
1347

Southern Russia
1345

From
Asia

*Atlantic
Ocean*

Mediterranean Sea

N

000 AD   1345-1349   1500 AD   2000 AD

*This map shows the devastating fourteenth-century migration of the
bubonic plague.*

powerless in the face of the Black Death. More disheartening in the nobility's case was the endless warfare of the knightly class contests that only added to the peasantry's woes.

The years ahead looked bleak indeed—a less-than-powerful church, a greedy nobility, seemingly endless wars, hunger, and illness. People wondered if it made sense to plan for any future at all amidst such horror and decay. It is no wonder, then, that the age at which men and women first married began to rise sharply. Couples delayed wedlock as long as they could, seeing no reason to join in each other's misery. Few people sought out attachments at a moment in history when attachments were so eas-ily severed. Families, when they were formed at all, were smaller than in the past because of declining birthrates. Either due to the higher ages at marriage, a reluctance to bring young ones into such a barren world, or some primitive form of contraception, fewer babies were being born by the late fourteenth century. Infanticide, or the killing of babies, was probably also practiced during this time. Disappointment and anxiety worsened the overall drop in Europe's population.

The number of adults remained abnormally low into the early fifteenth century. Land, no longer simply unused, was now often utterly abandoned. Local infrastructure such as roads, barns, mills, and forges fell to pieces. Entire villages

Causes and Cures

No one at the time knew what the bubonic plague was, why it spread, or how it killed. The state of European medical knowledge was not very advanced; it was dependent upon age-old and often ridiculous ideas about disease as caused by either an imbalance in bodily fluids, poisonous air, acts of God, or witchcraft. Doctors and patients alike could never have guessed that the Black Death was brought on by tiny animals transmitted from person to person due to flea bites. Nor could they have foreseen the interaction between illness, famine, and war. Furthermore, if some modern medical scholars are correct, other infectious diseases such as anthrax and typhoid might also have been at work in the fourteenth century, compounding the devastation wrought by *Y. pestis*. The ability to conceive of an epidemic due to a number of causes would not come about for another five hundred years or so. Thus Europeans did the best they could to cope with the unseen killer in their midst. They prayed, tortured and murdered Jews and suspected witches, and packed their pockets with flowers in the hope that the sweet aroma might overcome whatever poisonous gases carried the disease. Nothing worked. In the end, they simply suffered and died.

were deserted. Manors stood virtually empty. Once powerful lords suddenly found themselves in possession of empty, unworked, and hence worthless estates. As tenant farmers and serfs died or drifted away, manor lords sat by helplessly and watched their wealth, prestige, and authority vanish. They stood at the top of a social ladder that no longer had any lower rungs. In short, Georges Duby hardly exaggerated when he wrote that "the Black Death dealt a crushing blow to [feudalism's] already fragile demographic structure."[32]

The Reaction

The nobles attempted to resurrect some part of their former place in society by competing with one another for what was left of Europe's pool of farm labor. Putting into play an entirely new concept in labor relations, they offered to pay for work to be done. Peasants benefited from the novel farm-for-pay model. For the first time, their labor was truly valued, and they could negotiate for wages with which they could purchase their own land outright. Many serfs and tenants quickly became small, yet independent, farmers.

Freed from the mandatory service on the land, some common folk moved to Europe's cities, seeking to make the most of the emerging wage labor system. Cities, it followed, repopulated quickly, in some cases becoming larger than they had been before the Black Death. Urban businesses expanded and diversified in an economic setting awash in potential employees and consumers. Manufactur-

ing and construction picked up as workers' demands for food, clothing, and housing rose. The import-export market was rejuvenated by demand for staple goods as well as luxury items purchased by a growing urban elite. Businessmen and other prominent figures also enjoyed fresh political power as they took a guiding role in municipal affairs as mayors, councilmen, and other city officials. The Italian city-states, in particular, savored the fruits of urban growth combined with ready access to international markets. Sitting astride the lucrative trade routes that led from China and India into Europe, the Italian cities rapidly became the wealthiest and most influential of the fifteenth-century urban centers.

A Changing World

The Black Death altered the physical and social landscape of feudal Europe. True, the population eventually recovered, albeit slowly, and agricultural productivity reached and then surpassed pre-plague levels. The beliefs that had nurtured feudalism for so many centuries were no longer commonly found. The church, an important part of the feudal way of life, was losing its strength both politically and spiritually. Still reeling from the blow to its reputation dealt by the Muslims during the crusades, the church weakened itself further through a series of internal clashes. The worst of these quarrels resulted in the Great Schism, a period during which disputes over the rightful succession to the papacy led to the appearance of three rival popes. Each one of these men claimed to

The Blood Libel

Blaming Jews as being responsible for the Black Death was rooted in the deadly and persistent Jew-hatred that had been a part of Christian European culture since the second century. Considered to be the murderers of Jesus, Jews were believed to be the children of Satan, an alien and dangerous presence in the life of any community, it was thought. They were, therefore, accused of every crime and blamed for every misfortune imaginable. Jews were said to be the cause of crop failures, floods, droughts, and the inexplicable deaths of farm animals. So when a child disappeared, a common enough occurrence in a medieval world filled with physical dangers, Jews naturally came under suspicion. In 1144 vague fears that Jews occasionally kidnapped Christian boys formed the ridiculous myth known as the Blood Libel. Jews, it was claimed, snatched Christian boys, crucified them, and then used the innocents' blood for their Passover rituals. As cited in James Carroll's *Constantine's Sword: The Church and the Jews*, "It was laid down by [the Jews] in ancient times," so the story went, "that every year they must sacrifice a Christian in some part of the world." The Blood Libel was one of the reasons given for the persecution of Jews for the next eight centuries.

Quoted in James Carroll, *Constantine's Sword: The Church and the Jews*. Boston: Houghton Mifflin, 2001, p. 273.

be the legitimate head of the church and the heir to St. Peter (the first pope); each claimed to be the only true pope by divine inspiration.

The contest between the three popes made the papal authority seem less important. Many Christians doubted the authenticity of the church's assertion that it knew the will of God. Perhaps, some people wondered, the church is just a human institution, and a relationship with God was possible without it. Worse than the schism, though, was the church's inability to stop or at least explain the Black Death. If the priests and popes knew

God's will, why had they not been able to intercede to end the epidemic? Maybe, it was rumored, God did not speak through the church. Suspicion began to grow that the church might not be God's instrument on earth. After the violent suppression of a group of thirteenth-century reformers known as the Cathars, no one dared publicly to challenge the power of Rome, but some Europeans wondered if it was not time to rethink the church's role in spiritual life and its influence in politics and society.

Nobility, the other core feudal institution, was similarly damaged by the Black

Death and its companion disasters. The nobility never fully recovered from the disintegration of the manor system. Manor lords and the knights who owed them service became obsolete, seemingly in an instant. Titles such as duke, baron, and sir-this-or-that continued to be used, but the economic and political power implied by each had evaporated. If a landowner was lucky, he could transform himself into a country gentleman with lucrative business contacts and influence at the royal court. He might even take a bench in the increasingly assertive Parliament and help shape government policies. If he was unable to change with the times, a noble would find himself languishing as a relic of a bygone age.

The church and the nobility might have lost ground during the tumultuous and tragic fourteenth century, but Europe's kings gained it. Once akin to chief nobles, first among equals as it were, kings emerged out of the Black Death as newly invigorated political leaders. From around 1400 on, kings made aggressive moves to take control of the economies, legal apparatuses, and regional administrations within their realms. Monarchs, furthermore, fixed their attention on cities as sources of wealth that were independent of nobles and clergymen. Even in military matters kings began to assume the role of commander in chief, or sole master of their own armies. Feudal service began its evolution into royal service. In many ways, then, the Black Death heralded change on a continental scale in Europe. The age of feudalism had entered its twilight years.

Chapter Five

The Rise of the Nation-State

Summing up the changes that followed on the heels of the Black Death, the historian Lauro Martines wrote, "a new wind had arisen among the upper classes, a new set of values was sifting in to replace the old."[33] That wind, however, blew through the entire feudal structure, and its gusts fatally weakened the supports of a system that had survived for a thousand years. Yet it also cleared away the debris of post-crusades feudalism and opened Europe to novel ideas about how society and politics were supposed to work. Indeed, one of nature's tiniest creatures, the bacterium that caused the plague, did more to undermine the feudal way of life than any other single factor. *Yersinia pestis*, it could be said with confidence, helped alter world history and usher in the nation-state.

The population crash of the fourteenth century and the subsequent urban shift stripped the countryside of peasants and destroyed the manor system of agricultural production. To be sure, rural population figures rose again, however slowly, and farms continued to provide food for Europe. But the feudal mode of production, based as it was on the constant and ready availability of laboring hands, could not survive in an environment characterized by persistent labor shortages. Without serfs and tenant farmers, bound to the land by law and custom, manors simply could not function as they had in the past. Manor lords, forced to pay wages rather than allot grain as compensation for their dependents' work, had to accept a wholesale reshaping of local economies. Attempts by the nobility to forcibly recreate the old ways accomplished nothing. Many such efforts, in fact, resulted in violent uprisings such as the one that rocked England in 1381. The Peasants' Revolt and similar events in France and Italy demonstrated clearly that there was no turning back the clock.

The nobility's simultaneous failure to guarantee the safety of those below them in the feudal hierarchy only made matters worse. Whatever local power remained in its hands was dwindling rapidly. Common folk had presumed that the dukes, barons, and knights above them were at all times capable of offering protection to exposed and vulnerable villages and small towns. Armed defense by the nobility had been a key assumption of feudal theory. The belief was that protection came in exchange for obedience. The late-fourteenth century raids by ex-soldiers and roaming gangs of bandits upset this equation. Peasants forced to suffer through the violence quickly lost confidence in their lords. If the local elite could not provide for local security, then the bargain was off. The nobility's military obligations were clearly stated in the feudal social compact. The common people thus felt justified in withdrawing from the deal their ancestors had struck with the upper-class landowners.

After the devastation of the plague, many people were disillusioned by the power of the church, which led to the Peasants' Revolt in 1381.

In the minds of many, the church had similarly failed to live up to its feudal responsibilities. The fiasco of the crusades proved that the church, as a political and military institution, was far from all-powerful. Having been humbled by the armies of Islam, it was obvious that religious militancy had led to disaster. The church, it was whispered, did not have God on its side in the contest for the Holy Land. Nor did the pope and his clergy seem to have any special understanding of God's mind and will. The church had no solution to the riddle of the Black Death. It was unable to offer either comfort or hope as good Christians across Europe fell ill and died. As a result, challenges to the church's authority began to appear. As early as the 1370s, an English reformer named John Wycliff openly argued that the church's word was no longer final. More such voices were soon to follow.

The roles of the clergy and nobility in the feudal scheme of things, then, were fading speedily by the early fifteenth century, as was feudalism itself. Europe, in fact, was undergoing a complete reorientation away from popes and lords toward newly invigorated kings. Kings were emboldened and refreshed just as the age-old competitors for power were declining. An unmistakable trend toward centralization of authority in the monarchy became apparent. Kings felt confident enough to establish stronger and more effective royal bureaucracies, create military forces loyal exclusively to the crown, and exert control over trade and commerce. People began to assume identities as royal subjects, eclipsing older categories such as serf and lord. Men and women transferred their loyalty to distant kings and began sharing the monarchy's interests rather than those of local nobles and churchmen. The age of feudalism was fast approaching its end.

The Hundred Years' War

Feudalism was dying throughout Europe but nowhere faster than in England and France. The late fourteenth and early fifteenth centuries represented a transitional time during which a curious blend of feudal and modern institutions appeared. It was also a time of unrest and intense conflicts such as the extended period of warfare between England and France that was labeled the Hundred Years' War. Fought at a historical moment when, as J.F.C. Fuller put it, "kingdoms were rising into power [and] there was not sufficient room for two would-be dominant powers in Western Europe,"[34] the Hundred Years' War exemplified all of the changes overtaking Europe. The war itself was actually a long string of cross-Channel invasions by English armies bent on maintaining England's feudal claims to certain lands in France. Royal borders meant little at the height of the age of feudalism, but in its wake such borders came to mark out new national-cultural spheres. The pretensions of English kings thus became more than simply traditional noble claims; they were an assault by one sovereign kingdom against another, each with its own identity to protect. The two monarchies in question, to put it another way, were at war less than the French and English peoples they ruled over.

Although culturally significant, the Hundred Years' War turned out to be something of a stalemate, or at most a French victory in defense. It began in 1337, lasted until 1457, and had its share of famous battles. While many of these were classic feudal engagements (mounted knights in armor charging foot soldiers, archers, and enemy knights, all fighting

The Battle of Agincourt occurred during a time of intense conflict between England and France known as the Hundred Years' War.

out of feudal obligation to their lords), others pointed toward more modern forms of warfare. The two great battles of the war, Crécy (1346) and Poitiers (1356), are often cited as heralding the end of the era of armored knights. In both encounters English longbowmen decimated the French noble cavalry, proving that missile weapons could defeat heavily armored horsemen. Perhaps more important, the use of crude artillery at Crécy and later battles signaled a sea change in military technology and logistics. The manufacture of gunpowder and gunpowder weapons required resources far beyond those within the grasp of any single noble or group of nobles. Obtaining sulphur, saltpeter, and other minerals and combining them to form gunpowder was a huge undertaking, as was forging the gun tubes that would contain an explosion and use it to fire a projectile. Only a monarch with an entire kingdom to draw upon could manage the process of building artillery.

The employment of gunpowder weapons in war depended upon the creation and management of a production process that only a nation-state could handle. The use of such lethal tools in battle, especially against castles, further hastened the decline of feudalism. A king in possession of cannons could easily destroy his enemies, foreign and domestic alike. Nobles,

The *Encomienda* System

After claiming the New World for itself, Spain, in an odd twist of history, tried to export the dying institutions of feudalism to America. Lords, manors, and serfs were already relics in most parts of Europe by the time Spain invented a form of social organization known as the *encomienda* system. The basic outline of what was for a brief time the social model for Spanish America followed the rough contours of feudalism. Spanish adventurers, who went to America and served the crown's interests, were rewarded with land and people to work it. Men such as the discoverer of Florida, Juan Ponce de León, were given huge estates (*encomiendas*) and large numbers of Indian slaves on the condition that part of the income from those estates be given to the royal government. In effect, Spanish estate owners acted as manor lords with Indians as serfs. The *encomienda* holders acquired nearly unlimited legal authority over their workers and owed those below them only military protection. Due to racial prejudice, however, the New World version of feudalism was even more abusive than its European predecessor. As reports came in of torture and killing on the estates, complaints mounted. The Spanish government soon dismantled the *encomienda* system and ended its efforts to transplant feudalism to America.

once safe behind their castle walls, could now be forced into obedience. In earlier days, nobles could also indirectly threaten to withhold the soldiers needed for a king's military campaigns. Being intentionally tardy in calling his knights to their feudal obligation was one way in which a noble could assert himself. In an era of work-for-pay, however, kings by the late fourteenth century were already becoming accustomed to hiring troops. Nobles, indeed the entire feudal process called the levy, were essentially bypassed. Kings had the option now of raising armies by hiring men or using the armies they already possessed, armed with cannons, to compel a nobleman to supply needed soldiers. Royal armies, paid by and loyal to the king and his kingdom, had arrived. Such an innovation made the old ways obsolete. It is not surprising, then, to discover that the king of England issued his final call for a feudal levy in 1385. After that the English monarch recruited and paid his own forces.

Knights vulnerable in battle, nobles without castles, kings with their own armies—the years from 1337 to 1457 saw important changes in the way Europeans organized themselves for war and maintained the peace. The continent's monarchs took up positions at the head of governments strengthened by developments that weakened the nobility. More to the point, these royal governments, by uniting the previously fractured kingdoms and peoples of Europe behind the monarch, moved to the top of a new hierarchy built around loyalty not to a particular class of men but instead to the nation-state. The ancient social and political ties were being cut forever.

The Italian City-States and the "Citizen"

Feudalism was a tottering, decaying structure by the mid-1400s. It had failed again and again to meet history's challenges. From Spain to Scandinavia, as a consequence, powerful monarchies were moving to fill the void left by the old hierarchies. Only one place seemed to be immune to the monarchical alternative to feudalism, and that was Italy. Here, an entirely new relationship between the individual and the state was developing in city-states such as Genoa, Milan, Venice, and, above all, Florence. It was a relationship that diverged sharply from what came before it. In the cases of England and France, it could be argued that loyalty and duty to one man or woman, in the person of the king or queen, was a distant reflection of feudal bonds of obligation to a particular noble or pope. The same could not be said for Italy, where few if any vestiges of feudalism remained by 1400. Fueled by the philosophy of humanism, which placed an emphasis on individual liberty and service to one's native city, novel political structures had been built. Within these, the concept of the virtuous citizen was taking shape— a man so devoted to the welfare of his city and countrymen that he willingly put their interests above his own. The motive for this sacrifice, moreover, was simple love of country and community; in short, patriotism, or as it was known then, civic virtue.

Genoa, Italy, known for navigation and commerce, was one of the major Italian city-states in the Middle Ages.

As the idea of the citizen became ingrained, Italians in and near the major cities came together and formed themselves first into political associations and later into functioning republics. Elite control of the state was undiminished, of course, but the great men had new re-sponsibilities assigned to them under the republican system. They were expected, through their social and political lives, to serve the interests of the entire citizenry. The elite were also expected to ask for rather than demand authority. Elections, in this instance, provided the only legitimate avenue to power. An ambitious man might lean toward one faction or another within a particular city-state, since informal political parties existed throughout Italy, but at election time he had to present himself as a servant of the whole community. An insistence on secular, or nonreligious, government complemented the idea of the patriotic citizen. Civic virtue put a premium on public and private morality, so strong religious convictions were required of every citizen. But those convictions were not supposed to interfere with what was in a city's best political interests. Church and state were still viewed as a matched set, but a balance and a healthy degree of separation between them was considered essential. True enough, the church remained strong and quite influential in fifteenth-century Italy, but the future belonged to city-states that understood the difference between human and godly institutions.

Having denied the nobility and the clergy their traditional roles in the political order, the Italian city-state republics made room for men who claimed to have gained their positions in life through sheer merit. Only after years of demonstrated patriotism and selfless service could one claim the right to lead. The new republican political elite had to earn its place atop the hierarchy. Typical of this sort was the honest merchant who devoted himself to his business and dealt fairly with everyone. After making a name for himself through hard work and fair dealing, such a man might seek political office in the hope of bringing his

virtuous qualities to the policies of the city. The new political ideal placed a clear emphasis on citizens like this. Working for the good of their city and nothing else, the republican elite represented the best in every citizen and offered an example of what every citizen was expected to be.

Although radical in many respects, the notion of a citizenry in service to the republic had been evolving in Italy's city-states since at least the year 1200. Even before the republican model had been perfected, patriotism and citizenship had largely replaced feudal obligation and duty in Italian thinking. An Italian nobleman elected to office in Bologna in the early twelfth century, for example, accepted the job by pledging to do all in his power to ensure "the increase and glory of this glorious city and its citizens."[35]

The famous Florentine poet Dante Alighieri, writing in the early fourteenth century, asked himself in one volume of his trilogy, *The Divine Comedy*, whether "it would be worse for a man on earth were he not a citizen."[36] The reply was a hardy "Yes, and here I ask no reason."[37] Like most other Italians of his time, Dante took the role of citizen for granted. It was, put simply, a natural state of being.

For all this, only in the fifteenth century did the Italian republics mature into states in which citizenship became the measure of normality, signaling the death of feudalism there. Patriotism replaced feudal obligation; duty to the city-state replaced duty to the nobility and clergy. Italian writers, such as Leonardo Bruni, now spoke exclusively of *"vita activa-politica,"*[38] the politically active life of the citizen. Gone was the sense that only some people needed to be troubled by the responsibilities of government; every citizen was a leader. In this kind of climate feudal ideals seemed old-fashioned.

The New Way of War

In Italy and elsewhere in Europe feudalism stopped making sense by the fifteenth century. Its shortcomings and limitations in multiple facets of life had become painfully apparent. Yet perhaps its most glaring inadequacy came in an area that had always been its strong point—war. Feudalism's military side had been central to its overall success. The failure of the crusades had certainly called into question the value of feudal obligation as a way to organize and fight wars, but only in the fifteenth century did people conclude that feudalism had to be replaced. And here again, Italy led the way. From 1402 to 1454 the city-states fought each other for dominance on the Italian peninsula. Milan, Venice, Florence, and Pisa, in various combinations and alliances, battled incessantly for power. These wars were fought primarily with mercenary armies, whose soldiers were known as condottieri.

Essentially freelance warriors, the condottieri formed themselves into units-for-hire and fought for whomever paid

Henry the Navigator

Born in 1394 Henry was one of the six children of Portugal's King João I. He thus grew up in a climate of concern over how Europe would respond to the Muslim takeover of the Asian trade routes. Henry, unlike other men, reacted by embracing the challenge of finding new ways to access goods produced in China and India. He saw opportunity where others saw only a threat to the supply of needed imports from the East. Using the resources of the emerging Portuguese nation-state, Henry financed the first wave of European explorers charged with discovering alternatives to the traditional land routes made unusable by the Muslims. In doing so, the prince put Portugal at the leading edge of what some people call the age of exploration. Sailing with Henry's support and under his guidance, Portuguese explorers reached the Madeira Islands in 1418–1419 and claimed the Azores after a series of expeditions between 1427 and 1431. Later voyages carried Portuguese captains around the neck of Africa (Cape Verde) and into the Bight of Benin. These men were followed by others who explored and mapped the Senegal and Gambia rivers. Henry's efforts brought Portugal land and riches and made the tiny kingdom a world power.

Condottieri, such as Malatesta Baglione, were the first soldiers to fight for wages and rejected any kind of feudal obligation.

them. They lacked loyalty of any kind, especially to a particular city-state, but the condottieri also represented a complete rejection of any kind of feudal obligation. They were military men without a place in the social hierarchy and the first soldiers to fight for wages. In this sense the condottieri were quite modern. Even the fact that mercenaries were unpredictable and often uncontrollable had modern implications; the solution to the mercenary problem was the national army that continues in use to this day.

Across Europe feudal militaries were being abandoned. In France the Hundred Years' War displaced the nobility as the army's leading edge. The slaughter of so many knights at Crécy and Poitiers both reduced their total number and proved their uselessness in combat. By the time the war ended in 1457 a royal army had been created, an army loyal to the king and the French nation-state. A similar process took place in England, where civil war followed on the heels of the conflict with France. Called the Wars of the Roses (1455–1482), the individual wars were actually one great contest between the leading noble clans of England, the House of York and the House of Lancaster. When the conflict finally ended with a Lancastrian victory and the accession of Henry Tudor (Henry VII) to the throne, the new king moved aggressively to unite England and centralize power in the monarchy. Part of this process was to put the final touches on the establishment of a national English army that fought for king and country. As the sole commander in chief of the is-

land's soldiers, the English king, like his French counterpart, gained a monopoly on violence. The nobility lost its capability to physically challenge the crown. The nobility was reduced to waiting for favors to be doled out by a generous monarch or expressing its interests politically through debate in the halls of Parliament. Either way, it was clear that one nation under one king was the order of the day.

In France and England, the historian J.M. Roberts concluded, "war in the long run strengthened the monarchy."[39] It also produced a "sense of nationhood, [an] idea we take for granted."[40] Much the same could be said for Spain. Once a fractured and fragmented patchwork of noble holdings, Spain became a single kingdom, or a united nation-state, in 1479 when the twin kingdoms of Castile and Aragon were united. Ten years earlier the marriage of King Ferdinand of Aragon and Queen Isabella of Castile initiated the process of national unification, but war provided the glue that held the new Spanish state together. Ferdinand might easily exclaim on his wedding day, "Now . . . we are all brothers,"[41] proving that Spain's people were now one, after his marriage to Isabella, would be a more difficult proposition. Since the eighth century, war had raged on and off between Spain's Christians and Muslims. Both sides considered their ongoing contest to be a war for survival and the right to shape the Iberian peninsula's future. Over time the Christians gained the upper hand, slowly pushing their Islamic opponents back through central Spain to a small area around the city of Granada. Yet ultimate victory eluded the essentially feudal armies that fought to expel the Muslims. Nobles here and there might attain local success, but the gains could never be exploited. Only Spanish forces united under the new joint monarchy of Ferdinand and Isabella proved capable of completing that task. After centuries of war it took the armies of the new Spain a mere thirteen years to defeat the Muslims. In 1492 Granada fell, and the Spanish nation-state rose up.

The Nation-State and the Problem of Islam

Warfare highlighted the military inadequacies of the feudal system just as disease and famine had made apparent the shortcomings of its social aspects. The deficiencies of the nobility and the church could not be hidden from view after the catastrophes of the fourteenth century. Feudalism had undeniably failed as a way to organize Europe's societies and economies. It was fitting, then, that the old nemesis of the feudal period, Islam,

King Richard III promoted even stronger nation-states to fight Muslim forces.

should reappear on Europe's eastern borders in the mid-1400s.

In a certain sense the Muslim threat never truly receded. Europeans simply chose to disengage from it after the last of the major crusades ended in failure. The Muslims, however, kept pressing their advantage. After securing their undisputed control over the Holy Land, the Muslims presented new challenges in the East and in North Africa. Despite setbacks in Spain and subsequent coastal attacks by Spanish armies, North Africa's Muslims dug in and held their ground, denying any further inroads to the Christians. Islam's eastern branch, led by the Ottoman Turks, pressed forward against the Byzantine Empire, the only thing standing between the Muslims and another invasion of continental Europe. Already, in 1441–1442 the Turks had swarmed into Serbia and attacked Hungary only to be barely repulsed. The Turkish sultan's navy had been at war with Venice since 1416. By mid-century it appeared that only the remnants of the once-mighty Byzantine army kept Europe from feeling the full force of Islam's militancy. As long as the Byzantines absorbed most of the Muslim blows, the emerging nation-states were safe. Then suddenly in 1453 the Byzantine Empire fell to pieces. Constantinople fell to a Muslim army.

Now the Turks had to be met with unity and cohesion. This required even

Slavery and America

Serfdom, for all its degradation, was not the same as slavery. The feudal nobility might have liked to have the serfs reduced to slavery, but that was impossible for several reasons. First, serfs were Christians; they could claim the protection of the church. Second, serfs were Europeans and thus had a traditional role in society that shielded them against many abuses. Third, because of the first two reasons, the danger of uprisings hung over most manors. Pushed too far, serfs along with the rest of the peasantry might revolt, sending shock waves throughout society. Serfs, therefore, might have been at the bottom of the social order but they could not be owned and used as property. That changed with the discovery of the New World. Native Americans, like the Africans who suffered later, were neither Christian nor European, and because they did not have weapons like the Europeans, their revolts had no chance of ending slavery. Discovery and colonization offered an opportunity to redefine the relationship between land and labor. With nothing to stop them the European elite, supported by their nation-states, built a slave-labor system that would last for centuries and cost millions of lives.

stronger nation-states, commanding even greater loyalty from their peoples, noble and common alike. King Richard III of England certainly thought so. "I wish that my kingdom lay upon the confines of Turkey," he boasted. "With my own people alone and no other princes I should like to drive away . . . the Turks."[42] "My kingdom," Richard III called it, not the nobility's, not the church's. The English were no longer serfs and tenants who belonged equally to the king and the manor lords. The English were no longer simply Christians who owed their service and souls to the pope and his bishops. They were the king's people. They belonged to England. Feudalism's last breaths were being exhaled in Richard's words. The nation-state was drawing its first.

Chapter Six

The End of an Age

Coping with epidemic disease, recurring famine, and constant warfare would be difficult for any social system, especially one as sensitive to change as feudalism. European feudalism had been based on tradition, continuity, and most important, reliable population growth. From the sixth to the fourteenth centuries nothing had occurred that feudalism could not adapt to or adjust for, because nothing had dampened overall population increases. The Black Death and the other disasters of the fourteenth century were different. They effectively halted and, in many instances, reversed growth in the number of people living on the land, the one thing feudalism could not withstand. The result was a reengineering of the social hierarchy and the rise of the nation-state. Still, by the late 1400s some parts of the feudal system lingered in European society. The nation-state had made its debut; however, it was far from

mature. The European nobility continued to exert considerable influence in politics, and the church remained the continent's key cultural and spiritual institution. Land and religion still counted for much. Ironically, it would be a new land and a new religion that would snuff out the last embers of the feudal order and at last bring the age of feudalism to a close.

The Great Ocean Sea

Trade with Asia had figured prominently in Europe's economic life since the time of the Roman Empire. In fact, the Roman elite had developed an uncontrollable appetite for costly Asian imports, chief among them silk. Rome's collapse, therefore, was not surprisingly followed by a period during which the eastern trade routes fell into disuse. They became active again as Europe stabilized, and people once more began to consume Asian and South Asian products such as spices, pepper, dyes, exotic gems and hardwoods, and silk. By the eleventh and twelfth centuries, the decades that witnessed the crusades, East-West trade had become fully integrated into the European economy. The problem was that the main trade routes all passed through Muslim lands, corridors that could be closed easily as Islam asserted its dominance in the Middle East.

Throughout the fourteenth century the Ottoman Turks, in the territories they controlled, methodically shut down European trading stations, run mostly by merchants from the Italian city-states. By 1400 European access to the routes to Asia had been severely curtailed. Where access was granted by the Turks and others, merchants paid a heavy price in the form of taxes, bribes, and tribute to local strongmen. Costly and unreliable, the new difficulties in trading with China and India were compounded by the sea war between Venice and the Turks. Maneuvering the waters of the Mediterranean Sea became not only an expensive but also a dangerous proposition. And yet demand for eastern goods was unending. Consumption, in fact, was rising just as supply was falling. The need for new means of access to Asia became urgent. With the land routes constricted or closed altogether, only the sea lay open as an alternative.

Developing and maintaining ocean trade lanes to the East was far beyond anything a feudal Europe would have been capable of. Such an enterprise would require the kind of resources and organization that only a nation-state could provide. The Italian city-states, which had long controlled the old roads to Asia, might have been up to the challenge. They certainly had the resources to operate trading stations and finance and coordinate shipping, and they possessed fine merchant fleets. But the Italian city-states faced in the wrong direction. They looked toward the eastern Mediterranean and beyond to the old land avenues, such as the ancient Silk Road, for access to Asian products. With those avenues effectively closed, any new ones would be found through travel on the Atlantic Ocean. Opening, defending, and fully exploiting open-ocean routes would require capital investments, ships, and manpower beyond the means of places like Genoa and Venice. Italy's days as the center of European commerce and eastern trade were over.

Conquest and Colonization

Oceanic trade was more than the Italian city-states were capable of, largely due to simple geography: they were too small and in the wrong location. Other postfeudal states, however, were situated more advantageously and endowed with greater resources. England, France, Spain, and Portugal were already well into the transformation to fully fledged nation-states even before the shift of global commerce to the Atlantic; the opportunity to open Asian markets by sea completed the process. If feudalism was not dead already, it very soon would be. Portugal's successful establishment of a trade route around Africa's Cape of Good Hope to India in 1487, along with Spain's

settlement of the Americas after 1492, required that the two governments expand the scope of their involvement in what had become national projects of exploration and exploitation. Royal treasuries funded and royal bureaucracies managed the economies that developed in a global marketplace stretched from the Caribbean to the East China Sea.

England and France, due to wars both internal and external, got into the game slightly later, exploring and settling terri-

Christopher Columbus returns to the court of Ferdinand and Isabella of Spain in 1493 to tell of his discoveries in the New World.

did in the areas controlled by Portugal and Spain, but they would do so under the watchful eye and according to the dictates of national governments. More than one historian has concluded, as did Edward Potts Cheyney over a century ago when speaking of Spain, that "the position of the monarchs at home made easy and natural the adoption of their position of supreme patrons of the church [and their] entire freedom from dependence on the military and landed classes"[43] in the course of colonization.

In every case the basic process of conquest and colonization was the same and revealed the extent to which old feudal notions of power had been erased from European minds. Initial contact with some unknown or little-known place was followed by the establishment of permanent trading outposts and then colonies. These settlements required continued investment, resupply, defense, and proper administration. Central direction and funding, in other words, were crucial to success. Strong central authority guaranteed not only survival but also short- and long-term profitability. Nobles and clergymen were encouraged to become part of this process and were often rewarded with land and political influence. But this all came under a royal seal. The nobility and the church acted as agents of the monarchy rather than equals of it. No-

tories overseas only in the mid-sixteenth century. Their efforts, like those of their Spanish and Portuguese competitors, would nevertheless also represent national enterprises. The nobility and the church might become part of these projects, as they

bles could be stripped of their land; the church could be expelled from the colonies. The Atlantic kingdoms, as nation-states, ran the new worlds of trade and settlement. The old feudal notions about kings, nobles, the clergy, and power were now ridiculously out of date and functionally useless.

Christopher Columbus serves as an example of the new scheme of things. An Italian by birth, Columbus came from a long line of merchants and seafarers. As the commercial focus in Europe shifted to the Atlantic kingdoms, so did Columbus, offering his services first to Portugal and then Spain. It was for the king and queen of Spain that he sailed in 1492. And it was to those monarchs that Columbus gave the gold and slaves he took upon arrival in the New World. Only after his plan for a second voyage a year later had been finally approved by Ferdinand and Isabella did the Italian sailor discover that there were strings attached. The first trip had been more of a nation-state adventure than a money making enterprise; not so the second time around. Columbus was allowed to keep a mere 10 percent of any profit turned by his 1493 voyage; the rest went directly into the royal treasury. Considering that the crown was paying for the venture, Columbus was warned to keep strict accounts of where the national money went. The king and queen told their "Admiral of the Ocean Sea" to give clear instructions to the fleet's accountant: "You must see to it that he signs everything that is paid, since he must account for it to our inspector-general of taxes."[44] Far from the rugged adventurer of legend, Columbus

was in essence an agent of Spain. Although a lesser noble in his own right, Columbus was answerable to a royal bureaucracy and working in the national interest.

The Church and the New World

The men who came after Columbus—such as John Cabot, Vasco da Gama, Vasco Núñez de Balboa, and Juan Ponce de León—similarly worked as agents of the nation-state. None had the independence, let alone the power, of feudal nobles who would have filled their shoes just a hundred or two hundred years earlier. Without a doubt, the social and political role of the nobility had been redefined by the late fifteenth and early sixteenth centuries. Much the same could be said about the church. Renewed outbreaks of the plague and continuing internal disputes kept the church on the defensive in the fifteenth century. It struggled to answer fundamental questions about its spiritual credentials and common sense. Why, people asked, had the Holy Land been lost? Why was the church unable to intercede with God to bring health and peace to his children? How, during the Great Schism, could three men have claimed to be pope? The religious hierarchy struggled mightily to come up with plausible answers: The Lord acts in mysterious ways—perhaps. Humans are sinful and thus often punished—maybe. None of the church's explanations proved satisfactory. Deafening silence was the alternative.

The silence, however, had to be broken when news reached Europe of Christopher Columbus's startling dis-

Pope Alexander VI establishes the Line of Demarcation to define Spanish and Portuguese possessions in the New World on May 4, 1493.

The Wars of Religion

As the nation-state was being born, Europeans were busily killing one another in a series of local, regional, and continental wars of religion between Protestants and Catholics. During the sixteenth century both Germany and France were torn by extended bouts of violence between both religions. After Martin Luther's call for a more patriotic German Christian elite, the nobility in that country divided itself between his supporters and those of the pope and fought a vicious civil war that lasted until 1555. France suffered a similar fate until 1598. In England power changed hands between Catholics and Protestants from the 1540s until the late 1600s, transitions rife with purges, burnings, and beheadings. Religious violence gripped Europe as a whole from 1619 to 1648, as the Protestant kingdoms battled their Catholic opponents on the battlefields of central Europe. This conflict, known as the Thirty Years' War, ended with the Peace of Westphalia that declared the religion of a king to be that of his people. In effect, after 1648 the single church became many churches, each one nationalized to one extent or another. State religions arose to complement the political nation.

covery on the other side of the Great Ocean Sea. The Italian captain had stumbled upon a New World, an as yet unknown continent. It was a landmass inhabited by humans, and no one knew for sure how many or who they were. All anyone could say for certain was that neither the continent nor the people on it were supposed to exist. According to religious scholars and church teachings, every continent that existed, every place created by God, had already been found. Beyond those lands lay vast empty oceans, or so it was claimed. Yet here they were, land and the people to go with it, where neither should have been.

The church, once more, was confounded. Pope Alexander VI had to admit publicly that "our beloved son, Christopher Columbus . . . [has] discovered certain very remote islands and even mainlands that hitherto had not been discovered by others; wherein dwell many peoples living in peace."[45] The logical deduction, in many minds, was obvious. If this New World, America as it was called by 1506, had always been there, and the church had not known, it was because God had not told it. Nor, it seemed, had the Lord chosen to reveal the existence of millions of souls to his servants on earth. The only other explanation was that the church had simply been wrong, as it had been on so many important matters of late. More than a few thoughtful observers at the time wondered what else the church might be in error about.

The best the church leadership could come up with was to change the topic. Attempting to salvage some political influence just as it was losing its spiritual monopoly, the pope brokered a deal between Spain and Portugal to divide the Western Hemisphere between them. Although the Spanish and Portuguese kingdoms would have partitioned the New World anyway, with or without his mediation, the pope chose to add his name to the Treaty of Tordesillas (1494) and make himself appear to be more powerful than he was. Pope Alexander VI, working hard to seem an equal to the kings, even went so far as to warn Portugal and Spain that he would "lay his censures upon those who shall violate or oppose [the treaty] at any time whatsoever."[46] His words, however, rang hollow to monarchs who had long since recognized their own authority in political affairs.

The last-ditch effort on the part of the church to regain the initiative involved the categorization of the people Columbus had found living so peacefully in America. Responding to questions concerning the church's relationship to so many souls as yet unaware of it or the God it served, the hierarchy panicked and claimed that the Native Americans were not human. This assertion filled two needs. One, if the Indians were not human they could be enslaved and set to work supplying the Portuguese and Spanish with the gold and silver each kingdom craved.

This might earn the favor of the monarchies. Two, if they were not human, then the church had never been wrong about their presence in the first place. The church never said that all the types of animals in the world had been discovered. It was a transparent attempt to prop up the church's sagging fortunes.

But it failed. Due to the efforts of churchmen such as Bartolomé de Las Casas, the church was forced to acknowledge the humanity of the people Columbus found in

Spanish missionary and historian Bartolomé de Las Casas argued for the church to recognize the humanity of Indians in America.

America. In a display of courage and forthrightness that would not have been possible at the height of the church's power during the age of feudalism, Las Casas stepped forward to argue the Indian case. Quoting liberally from ancient philosophy, Las Casas based his defense on the very modern idea that "all the peoples of the world are men; and there is only one definition of each and every man, and that is that he is rational."[47] When his opponents labeled the Indians as savages and barbarians, Las Casas replied, "we are just as barbarous to them as they to us."[48] In 1542 the church relented and proclaimed Native Americans to be full members of the human community. It seemed that they too were God's children.

The Protestant Reformation

Hammered by Las Casas's arguments concerning the spiritual status of Native Americans, the church gave in. The pope and the rest of the religious hierarchy in Rome had no energy to waste in a point-

Martin Luther, the Protestant Reformation, and the Nation-State

Martin Luther's initial protest concerned the church practice of issuing certificates called indulgences. Indulgences allowed a person to speed a departed loved one's way into heaven by pardoning them for their sins in this life. Luther's opposition to selling tickets to heaven, however, soon evolved into a more general argument against the idea that good deeds were as important as faith in one's relationship with God. Along the way, Luther challenged the role of the pope in Christian life. In 1517 Luther openly made his views clear on both subjects when he nailed his protests to the doors of the cathedral in Wittenburg, Germany. Ordered by the pope to retract his words, Luther refused. He was thus promptly excommunicated, or expelled, from the church in 1520. That same year he published a pamphlet titled *An Open Letter to the Christian Nobility of the German Nation Concerning the Reform of the Christian Estate.* In it Luther urged the German nobles to defend their nation "or Germany will soon be like Italy," under the heel of a corrupt pope. He claimed that church officials waited to pounce on "Germany as wolves lie in wait for sheep." (Both quotes from John L. Beatty and Oliver A. Johnson, eds., *Heritage of Western Civilization.*) Luther, therefore, called upon Germans to stand up for Germany and religious reform. God and country, for the first time, became one.

Quoted in John L. Beatty and Oliver A. Johnson, eds., *Heritage of Western Civilization,* vol. 1. Englewood Cliffs, NJ: Prentice-Hall, 1987, p. 438.

Martin Luther challenged the role of the pope in Christian life and was excommunicated, or expelled, from the church in 1520.

less debate they were sure to lose. Other matters far more pressing and troubling occupied their minds in the early sixteenth century. A far more dangerous challenge to church authority and the supremacy of the pope had arisen in Germany. There, a reform movement led by a renegade priest, Martin Luther, threatened to split the church in two. Luther claimed that a Christian could have a personal relationship with God, one based solely on faith. This claim ran counter to the Catholic belief that salvation depended upon faith being combined with good works. Luther's belief defied the power of Rome and held that the pope was not God's representative on earth.

Within ten years Luther's protest movement evolved into the Protestant Reformation. From Germany, Luther's radical views and calls for a new religion spread to France, Switzerland, England, and Scandinavia. Luther's words of defiance were amplified and refined by other men such as John Calvin and

Huldrych Zwingli. By the time Las Casas took up the Indian cause, much of northern Europe had abandoned the church, now referred to as the Roman Catholic Church to distinguish it from its Protestant enemies. King Henry VIII of England had gone so far as to create his own branch of Christianity, known as the Church of England, and placed himself at its head. This was the ultimate subordination of the clergy. The king of a nation-state had made himself the religious leader of his people as well. Church and state were no longer partners; the church was now effectively a branch of the government.

Nor was Henry alone. Throughout northern Europe, Protestant churches were forming and placing themselves at the service of the state. Where they remained unchallenged or predominant for the time being, Catholic churches were doing likewise. As they battled for the hearts, minds, and souls of Europeans, both Catholics and Protestants desperately needed political allies for protection and support. The physical safety and long-term success of each religion depended on its ability to secure the assistance of kings and princes. Across Europe, churches reached out to national leaders. Depending upon where they were located, Catholic and Protestant establishments were transformed from independent agencies into national churches. Someone who had once been simply a Christian obeying the dictates of the pope in Rome now became a Spanish Catholic or a German Protestant and so forth. Church leaders aligned themselves with national leaders and national agendas. Religion was thus secondary to the new

nation-states in a way no feudal churchman or layperson could have dreamed.

An Age Remembered

The last wisps of feudalism drifted away forever by the mid-seventeenth century. The centralized nation-state was triumphant. Absolute and limited monarchies governed Europe, monarchies that took for granted the unrivaled power of the state. Yet even in small countries without kings, such as Switzerland and Holland, ultimate authority belonged to the state rather than the nobility or clergy as a social and political class. Remnants of feudal obligation lingered only in remote parts of far Russia, and even there they would soon be under attack as signs of backwardness.

The Catholic Church no less than the nobility had been humbled. Its continental power had been broken, and it came to be seen as inferior compared to the state. The Peace of Westphalia (1648), which ended the last of the religious wars in Europe, enshrined the principle that the government had the right to determine its citizens' religion. Although the notion of freedom of religion would emerge within another hundred years, the assumption would be that individuals were at liberty to choose their own faith. Europeans came to assume that either governments or citizens made such spiritual decisions. The churches simply responded with the appropriate services.

In every facet of life, feudalism was gone. Land became just land, most of it owned by the state; money was power, money made by individual citizens who

Japanese Feudalism

A form of feudalism developed very early in Japan. Beginning in the late eleventh century, feudal ideas and institutions evolved to meet the needs of an island empire beset by war and instability. By 1185 feudalism was the social order of the day. The similarities between Japanese and European feudalism were as striking as the differences. In Japan as in Europe, nobles functioned as manor lords who dominated the agricultural peasantry. The manor lords (daimyo) owed service upward to the emperor, or more often the shogun (a noble warlord who acted as regent and usually dominated the emperor), and received service from a knightly class, the samurai. The nobility, just as in Europe, was supported by serfs bound to the land, who grew Japan's food. Warfare between Japanese nobles was a chronic problem that necessitated the construction of fortified estates centered around castle complexes. The primary difference between the two variants was Japanese feudalism's resilience. Unlike its European counterpart, the Japanese version of feudalism did not collapse and give birth to the nation-state. In Japan feudalism survived into the nineteenth century and was replaced only when the nation-state format was imposed upon it by, of all people, the Europeans and Americans.

might or might not be titled as nobility. People were subjects of the king or citizens of the republic, but they were no longer serfs or tenants under the heel of a local noble. Obligations were standardized by laws, laws that collected people together under national codes. Although their social privileges and prerogatives remained vastly different, the elite and the commoners were governed by legal systems and political administrations.

The age of feudalism thus ended as it had begun—out of practical necessity. Decentralized power and bonds of personal duty and obligation revolving around landholding and agricultural production arose out of the ashes of the Roman Empire to meet the pressing needs of the post-imperial world. They were an attempt to reestablish order and stability where it had disintegrated. Feudal institutions were both rational and effective at the time, but by the sixteenth and seventeenth centuries their day had long passed. War, disease, and religious conflict required novel forms of government and social organization. Fresh ideas and outlooks were required that rejected everything on which feudalism had been based. Knights and castles, serfs and lords, simply faded away as feudalism, exhausted and empty, met its end.

Notes

Introduction: Rome, A.D. 410

1. Quoted in David Willis McCullogh, ed., *Chronicles of the Barbarians: First-hand Accounts of Pillage and Conquest, from the Ancient World to the Fall of Constantinople.* New York: History Book Club, 1998, p. 143.

2. Morris Bishop, *The Middle Ages.* Boston: Houghton Mifflin, 1968, p. 9.

3. Bishop, *The Middle Ages*, p. 10.

Chapter One: Barbarian Kingdoms

4. Antonio Santosuosso, *Storming the Heavens: Soldiers, Emperors, and Civilians in the Roman Empire.* Boulder, CO: Westview, 2001, p. 8.

5. Quoted in J.M. Wallace-Hadrill, *The Barbarian West, 400–1000.* New York: Barnes & Noble, 1967, p. 69.

6. John Julius Norwich, *A Short History of Byzantium.* New York: Alfred A. Knopf, 1997, p. 68.

Chapter Two: Charlemagne to Clermont

7. Quoted in Bishop, *The Middle Ages*, p. 23.

8. Quoted in Bishop, *The Middle Ages*, p. 25.

9. Quoted in Antonio Santosuosso, *Barbarians, Marauders, and Infidels: The Ways of Medieval Warfare.* Boulder, CO: Westview, 2004, p. 142.

10. Quoted in McCullogh, *Chronicles of the Barbarians*, p. 215.

11. Oliver Lyman Spaulding and Hoffman Nickerson, *Ancient and Medieval Warfare.* New York: Barnes & Noble, 1993, p. 259.

12. Quoted in Santosuosso, *Barbarians, Marauders, and Infidels*, pp. 146–47.

13. Quoted in Spaulding and Nickerson, *Ancient and Medieval Warfare*, p. 287.

14. Quoted in Richard Fletcher, *The Barbarian Conversion: From Paganism to Christianity.* New York: Henry Holt, 1997, p. 433.

Chapter Three: The Church Militant

15. Quoted in McCullogh, *Chronicles of the Barbarians*, p. 323.

16. Quoted in McCullogh, *Chronicles of the Barbarians*, pp. 324–25.

17. Quoted in McCullogh, *Chronicles of the Barbarians*, pp. 324–25.

18. Quoted in Bishop, *The Middle Ages*, p. 77.

19. John A. Lynn, *Battle: A History of Culture and Conflict from Ancient Greece*

to *Modern America*. Cambridge, MA: Westview, 2003, p. 78.

20. Georges Duby, *Rural Economy and Country Life in the Medieval West*, trans. Cynthia Postan. Columbia: University of South Carolina Press, 1968, p. 183.

21. Quoted in Zoé Oldenbourg, *The Crusades*, trans. Anne Carter. London: Weidenfeld and Nicholson, 1966, p. 83.

22. Quoted in McCullogh, *Chronicles of the Barbarians*, p. 341.

23. Quoted in McCullogh, *Chronicles of the Barbarians*, p. 346.

24. Quoted in Karen Armstrong, *Holy War: The Crusades and Their Impact on Today's World*. New York: Anchor, 1988, p. 199.

25. Quoted in James Reston Jr., *Warriors of God: Richard the Lionheart and Saladin in the Third Crusade*. New York: Doubleday, 2001, p. 82.

Chapter Four: The Black Death

26. Quoted in Bishop, *The Middle Ages*, p. 179.

27. Quoted in R.S. Bray, *Armies of Pestilence: The Impact of Disease on History*. New York: Barnes & Noble, 1996, p. 49.

28. Quoted in Bray, *Armies of Pestilence*, p. 49.

29. Quoted in Bray, *Armies of Pestilence*, p. 61.

30. Barbara Tuchman, *A Distant Mirror: The Calamitous Fourteenth Century*. New York: Alfred A. Knopf, 1978.

31. Quoted in James Carroll, *Constantine's Sword: The Church and the Jews*. Boston:

Houghton Mifflin, 2001, p. 339.

32. Duby, *Rural Economy and Country Life*, p. 308.

Chapter Five: The Rise of the Nation-State

33. Lauro Martines, *Power and Imagination: City-States in Renaissance Italy*. Baltimore: Johns Hopkins University Press, 1979, p. 170.

34. J.F.C. Fuller, *A Military History of the Western World: From the Earliest Times to the Battle of Lepanto*. New York: De Capo, 1954, p. 446.

35. Quoted in Martines, *Power and Imagination*, p. 125.

36. Quoted in R.W.B. Lewis, *Dante*. New York: Viking, 1995, p. 68.

37. Quoted in Lewis, *Dante*, p. 69.

38. Quoted in Peter Riesenberg, *Citizenship in the Western Tradition: From Plato to Rousseau*. Chapel Hill: University of North Carolina Press, 1992, p. 189.

39. J.M. Roberts, *A History of Europe*. New York: Allen Lane, 1996, p. 177.

40. Roberts, *A History of Europe*, p. 173.

41. Quoted in J.H. Elliot, *Imperial Spain, 1469–1716*. New York: Penguin, 1963, p. 24.

42. Quoted in Margaret Aston, *The Fifteenth Century: The Prospect of Europe*. New York: W.W. Norton, 1968, p. 106.

Chapter Six: The End of an Age

43. Edward Potts Cheyney, *European Background of American History*,

1300–1600. 1904; repr. New York: Frederick Ungar, 1978, p. 107.

44. Quoted in Björn Landström, *Columbus: The Story of Don Cristóbal Colón, Admiral of the Ocean, and His Four Voyages Westward to the Indies*. New York: Macmillan, 1966, p. 108.

45. Quoted in Henry Steele Commager, ed., *Documents of American History*, vol. 1. New York: Appleton-Century-Crofts, 1958, p. 3.

46. Quoted in Commager, *Documents of American History*, p. 4.

47. Quoted in J.H. Elliott, *The Old World and the New, 1492–1650*. New York: Cambridge University Press, 1970, p. 48.

48. Quoted in Elliott, *The Old World and the New*, p. 49.

For More Information

Books

Geoffrey Barraclough, *The Crucible of Europe: The Ninth and Tenth Centuries in European History*. Berkeley: University of California Press, 1976. Barraclough provides an excellent discussion of the centuries during which feudal Europe was forged.

Frances Gies, *Cathedral, Forge, and Waterwheel: Technology and Invention in the Middle Ages*. New York: HarperCollins, 1994. Gies dispels the myths surrounding the medieval use of technology, proving that people during the Middle Ages were quite advanced in terms of the tools and machinery they used.

Jacques Le Goff, *Medieval Civilization, 400–1500*. New York: Oxford University Press, 1988. Le Goff offers a fine general overview of the history of the Middle Ages.

Paul B. Newman, *Daily Life in the Middle Ages*. Jefferson, NC: McFarland, 2001. Newman's book examines the lives of kings, bishops, and ordinary people alike as they went about their daily business.

Walter Ullmann, *The Individual and Society in the Middle Ages*. Baltimore: Johns Hopkins University Press, 1966.

Web Sites

The End of Europe's Middle Ages: Feudal Institutions (www.ucalgary.ca/applied_history/tutor/endmiddle/feudal.html). This site looks at the various institutions that allowed feudal Europe to function and flourish. It also considers how those institutions figured in the transition from medieval to early modern Europe.

Feudalism (www.blackstudies.ucsb.edu/antillians/feudalism.html). This site provides a very useful discussion of feudalism as a social, cultural, and political system.

Feudalism in Europe: An Overview (http://history-world.org/feudalism2.htm). A solid general survey of feudalism is found here.

Feudalism and Knights in Medieval Europe (www.metmuseum.org/toah/hd/feud/hd_feud.htm). The relationship between the feudal system and the men who defended it is outlined at this site. Knights, as a class and as individuals, are the focus of attention.

History of Feudalism (www.historyworld.net/wrldhis/PlainTextHistories.asp?historyid=ac35). A general history of feudalism, in all its forms, is at this site. The early history of the system is very well described.

Index

Picture Credits

About the Author

John Davenport holds a Ph.D. in History from the University of Connecticut and is the author of numerous books on subjects ranging from biography to historical geography. His published works include a history of the Nuremburg war crimes trials and a biography of the medieval Muslim leader Saladin. Davenport lives in San Carlos, California, with his wife, Jennifer, and his two sons, William and Andrew.